WORK EDITION

Skills in
ENGLISH

3 G

Lindsay McNab

Imelda Pilgrim

Marian Slee

Literacy consultant: Jacqui Buckley

Heinemann

The authors and publishers would like to thank Bernadette Pearce for writing Section F – Words: spelling strategies and vocabulary. They would also like to extend grateful thanks to David Robinson for his work as Grammar Consultant on the series.

Heinemann Educational Publishers
Halley Court, Jordan Hill, Oxford OX2 8EJ
Part of Harcourt Education

Heinemann is a registered trademark of Harcourt Education Limited

First published 2002
06   05   04   03
10   9   8   7   6   5   4   3   2

ISBN 0 435 19288 4

Designed by 320 Design. Produced by Gecko Ltd, Bicester, Oxon
Printed and bound in Italy by Printer Trento S.r.l.

Picture research by Jennifer Johnson

Original illustrations © Heinemann Educational Publishers 2002

The publishers would like to thank the following for permission to reproduce photographs on the pages noted:

BBC, pp.34, 37; Jackie Chapman/Format, p. 138; Corbis, pp.61, 117-8; Dahl and Dahl, pp.87-8; Express Syndication, pp.107-9; Eye Ubiquitous, p. 121; Melanie Friend, p. 91; Gavin Hellien, p. 120; Honeywell, p.57; Peter Merten, p. 120; Peter Morris, p. 137; Peter Newark, pp.129, 131-2; Photodisc, pp.103 and 105; Popperfoto, p. 164; UPPA, pp.107-9; Vanderhast/Robert Harding, p.56; V. Young, p.120.

Illustrations: Chris Brown, Abigail Conway, David Cuzik, Nick Duffy, Alice Englander, Teresa Flavin, Tony Forbes, Phil Healey, Rosalind Hudson, Paul McCaffrey, Chris Molan, Julian Mosedale, Kathryn Prewett, Andy Quelch, Mary-Claire Smith, Jennifer Ward.

Permissions sought by Jackie Newman

Tel: 01865 888058   www.heinemann.co.uk

Introduction

Prometheus Unbound

He gave man speech, and speech created thought,
Which is the measure of the universe.

*from **Prometheus Unbound** by P. B. Shelley*

AS YOU HAVE developed your skills in English you have become more aware of the power of words. You have started to recognise the influence words can have. You have learned to read words with greater understanding and to use them more effectively in your own speech and writing.

Alongside this recognition of the power of words you need to be aware of the importance of thought. Skilled readers do not always believe everything they read. They ask questions, think about effects and search for the right words to express an idea. When speaking they listen to others with an awareness of tone and match this when replying. In writing they spend time gathering ideas and working out how they are going to get these across to their readers. The brain is always active and lively, challenging new ideas, bringing personal experience to a text ... thinking.

The texts and activities in this book have been selected to help you develop your skills in English. As you work your way through the units be prepared to question and to challenge the content. The answers are often not on the page but in your head, and the more thought you give to your work the better your progress will be.

The following icons are used in this book:

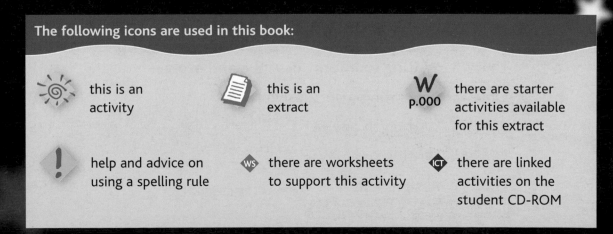

this is an activity

this is an extract

W p.000 there are starter activities available for this extract

help and advice on using a spelling rule

ws there are worksheets to support this activity

ICT there are linked activities on the student CD-ROM

CONTENTS

Section E – Speaking and listening — 159

Section F – Words: spelling strategies and vocabulary — 195

ACKNOWLEDGEMENTS

The publishers gratefully acknowledge the following for permission to reproduce copyright material. Whilst every effort has been made to locate the owners of copyright, in some cases this has proved unsuccessful. The publishers apologise for any omission of original sources and will be pleased to make the necessary arrangements at the first opportunity.

Extract from list of 'knave insults' from *Shakespeare's Insults* by W. F. Hull and G. F. Ottchen published by Ebury, London, p.13. Extract from *Holes* by Louis Sachar published by Bloomsbury Children's Books 2000: reprinted by permission of Bloomsbury Publishing plc, p.16. *The Breadwinner* by Leslie Howard Copyright © Leslie Howard, pp.19–21. 'The Caged Bird in Springtime' by James Kirkup from *A Correct Compassion and Other Poems* published by Oxford University Press in 1954 and also in *Collected Shorter Poems Vol 1* published by Salzburg Press 1997 Copyright © James Kirkup: reprinted with the kind permission of the author, p.30. 'A Constable Calls' by Seamus Heaney from *New Selected Poems* published by Faber and Faber Limited: reprinted with permission of Faber and Faber Limited, p.33. 'Stereotype' by John Agard from *Mangoes and Bullets* published by Pluto Press 1985 Copyright © John Agard 1985: reprinted by kind permission of John Agard c/o Caroline Sheldon Literary Agency, p.38. 'Dress Sense' by David Kitchen Copyright © David Kitchen: reprinted with the kind permission of the author, p.42. 'Dread-lock style' by Lesley Miranda found in *Poetry Jump Up* published by Puffin, p.43. Extract from *Whispers in the Graveyard* by Theresa Breslin published by Mammoth Copyright © Theresa Breslin 1994: reprinted by permission of Laura Cecil Literary Agency on behalf of Theresa Breslin, p.46. Extract from *Throwaways* by Ian Strachan Copyright © Ian Strachan: reprinted by permission of Ian Strachan c/o Caroline Sheldon Literary Agency, p.46. Extract from 'Pawley's People' from *The Starlit Corridor* by John Wyndam: reprinted by permission of David Higham Associates Limited, p.47. Extract from *Kit's Wilderness* by David Almond published by Hodder 1999 © David Almond: reproduced by permission of Hodder & Stoughton Limited, p.47. Extract from *The Giver* by Lowis Lowry, published by Collins 1999 Copyright © Lowis Lowry 1999: reprinted by permission of HarperCollins Publishers, p.47. 'Smart Ice-Cream' by Paul Jennings from *Unreal!* published by Penguin Australia: reprinted with permission of the publishers, pp.48–51. Extract from the *Escape* section of the *Observer*, 12th August, 2001 (a piece on phrase books by Joanne O'Connor) Copyright © The Observer: used with permission, pp.56–7. Extract from *Neither Here Nor There* by Bill Bryson © Bill Bryson, published by Blackswan, a division of Transworld Publishers; all rights reserved: used by permission of the publishers, p.61. Excerpt from *Travels With Fortune: An African Adventure* by Christina Dodwell (London: W. H. Allen/Virgin Publishing 1979) Copyright © Christina Dodwell: reprinted with kind permission of the author, p.64. 'Poem Against Capital Punishment' by Roger McGough from *Defying Gravity* published by Penguin Books, Copyright © Roger McGough: reprinted by permission of Peters Fraser & Dunlop on behalf of Roger McGough, p.66. 'Cinquain' by Valerie Bloom © Valerie Bloom first published in *The Works* published by Macmillan: reprinted by kind permission of the author, p.67. 'Who is de Girl?' by John Agard from *No Hickory, No Dickory, No Dock* published by Viking 1990 Copyright © John Agard 1990: reprinted by permission of John Agard c/o Caroline Sheldon Literary Agency. Extract from *Cider with Rosie* by Laurie Lee published by Hogarth Press: used by permission of The Random House Group Limited, p.75. Cover of 'John Barnes' autobiography published by Hodder & Stoughton Limited (Photo © Jean-Francois Talivez): reprinted with the kind permission of Jean-Francois Talivez and Hodder & Stoughton Limited, p.77. Cover of 'Long Walk to Freedom' Nelson Mandela published by Little Brown & Co, p.77. Extract from *Falling Leaves Return to Their Roots: The True Story of an Unwanted Chinese Daughter* by Adeline Yen Mah (Michael Joseph 1997) Copyright © Adeline Yen Mah 1997: reprinted by permission of Penguin Books Limited, p.78–9. Extract from *All Points North* by Simon Armitage (Viking 1998) Copyright © Simon Armitage 1998: reprinted by permission of Penguin Books Limited, pp.82–3. Extract from *Lark Rise to Candleford* by Flora Thompson (1945) published by Oxford University Press: reprinted by permission of Oxford University Press, p.84–6. Extract from *Going Solo* by Roald Dahl published by Jonathan Cape and Penguin Books: reprinted by permission of David Higham Associates Limited, p. 88. 'Clear Complexion Advert' reprinted with the kind permission of Jessup Marketing, p.91. Extract from 'Frog Tours leaflet' reprinted with the kind permission of Frog Tours, pp.76 and 93. WDCS banner: reprinted with the kind permission of WDCS (Whale and Dolphin Conservation Society), p.91. Two adverts and an extract from the Barnardo's website: reprinted with the kind permission of Barnardo's, pp.96 and 98. 'Rumble in the Countryside' by Joanne Murphy, from *The Stockport Express*: reprinted with permission, p.108. Extract from *I Know Why The Caged Bird Sings* by Maya Angelou published by Virago Copyright © Maya Angelou: reprinted by permission of Time Warner Books UK, pp.111–3. Various extracts from *The Mysterious Case of the Mary Celeste* published by Tressell Publications 1981, pp.123–4. Extracts from *The Score: Facts about Drugs*: reproduced by permission of Health Promotion England, p.135. 'Thunder and Lightning' by James Kirkup from *The Prodigal Son: Poems 1956–1959* (Oxford University Press) Copyright © James Kirkup: reprinted with kind permission of the author, p.152. 'The Listeners' by Walter de la Mare, from *The Complete Poems of Walter de la Mare 1969*: reprinted by permission of The Literary Trustees of Walter de la Mare and the Society of Authors as their representative, p.154. Blue Cross logo and text: reprinted with the kind permission of the Blue Cross, p.156. Extract from *Higher than Hope: A Biography of Nelson Mandela* by Fatima Meer (Hamish Hamilton 1990) Copyright © Fatima Meer 1990, p.164. Extract from *Blood Brothers* by Willy Russell published by Methuen: reprinted by permission of Methuen Publishing Limited, pp.169–70 and 172–3. Extracts from *Stone Cold* by Robert Swindells (Hamish Hamilton 1993) Copyright © Robert Swindells 1993: reprinted by permission of Penguin Books Limited, pp.176–7 and 180.

Section A ◆ Reading literature
Introduction

In this book the word 'literature' is used to describe the range of written material that is linked with the imagination and making things up. This includes prose, which may be short stories or novels, poetry or play scripts.

In Year 8 you will have developed your understanding of genre and your awareness of writers' techniques. You will have explored literature from different cultures, and thought about some of the differences between standard English and dialect.

You will be building on these skills in the three units of work in this section.

In Unit 1, *Appreciating variety in language*, you will develop your understanding of how language is used and how it changes over time. You will think about the variety and richness of language and relate major writers to their historical context.

In Unit 2, *Reading in depth*, you will examine a text closely. You will learn how to interpret detail and refer to the text when answering questions. You will identify similarities and differences between characters, and develop your skills in writing about these.

In Unit 3, *Recognising the writer's stance*, you will consider how different writers present their ideas. You will compare the themes and styles of two poets, and will learn to distinguish between the attitudes of characters and those of the writer.

Unit 4 tests you on the skills you will develop as you work carefully through the three units.

This unit will help you to:

- understand that language changes over time
- develop your understanding of how language works
- link well-known writers to the time when they wrote
- recognise some features of highly regarded texts.

How English has changed

Old English

Do you recognise the language used in the extract below? Try reading it aloud. The 'þ' is called a thorn and is pronounced 'th'. In pairs, discuss words that you think you recognise or can guess at.

The Battle of Maldon

p.198

Her lið ure ealdor eall forheapen,
god on greote. A mæg gnornian
se ðe nu fram þis wigplegan wendan þenceð.
Ic eom frod feores. Fram ic ne wille,
5 ac ic me be healfe minum hlaforde,
be swa leofan men licgan þence.

from **The Battle of Maldon**, *Old English poem*

In fact, the language is a very old form of English that was once spoken and written. This extract is taken from a poem about the Battle of Maldon, fought more than one thousand years ago in AD 991 between the English and the Vikings. This type of English is called Old English or Anglo-Saxon.

In AD 449, 542 years before this poem was written, Saxons, Angles and Jutes from powerful German nations had started to invade England. They brought their language with them and many words still used in English today are of German origin.

When trying to work out the meaning of Old English, look for clues in the words:

Shares the same first three letters as 'here', or could mean 'she'.

Contains the word 'all'.

Does this remind you of 'in a heap'?

Her lið ure ealdor eall forheapen,

A bit like 'elder', a person of senior position.

This will help you to reach the line's actual meaning: ' Here lies our chief all cut down'.

Activity 1 ICT

1 Re-read the first line of the extract opposite. Which two words can you match with these German words?

    a hier (German: here)   **b** unser (German: our)

2 By using what you know about word patterns, try to work out the Old English equivalent for these modern English words:

from (line 3)   I (line 4)   of my (line 5)   man (line 6)
this (line 3)   years (line 4)   by (line 6).

3 Now check your guesses against this recent translation of these lines:

> Here lies our chief all cut down,
> a noble man in the dust. He has reason ever to mourn
> who intends now to turn from this war-play.
> I am advanced in years. I will not leave,
> but I by the side of my lord,
> by so dear a man, intend to lie.

Middle English

In 1066 the Battle of Hastings was won by William the Conqueror. He was from Normandy in France and brought his language to Britain. It is thought that some 10,000 French words came into English at that time.

The language of this period is called Middle English. One of its most famous writers was Geoffrey Chaucer (about 1343–1400) whose best known work is *The Canterbury Tales*. Chaucer writes about a band of pilgrims who are people on a religious journey. They agree to liven up their journey with a story-telling competition.

In the extract on page 10, Chaucer introduces one of the pilgrims, the Wife of Bath.

To help the reader understand the language, editors of Old and Middle English texts use footnotes to:

- ◆ explain the meanings of some of the words
- ◆ give extra useful information.

These notes are usually placed at the bottom of a page.

Activity 2 (ws)

Here are the footnotes for the extract below. The words and their meanings have been mixed up. Read the extract, then try to match the words in **bold** to the correct meanings. Some have been done for you.

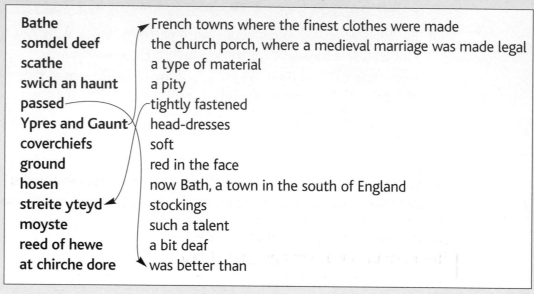

Bathe	French towns where the finest clothes were made
somdel deef	the church porch, where a medieval marriage was made legal
scathe	a type of material
swich an haunt	a pity
passed	tightly fastened
Ypres and Gaunt	head-dresses
coverchiefs	soft
ground	red in the face
hosen	now Bath, a town in the south of England
streite yteyd	stockings
moyste	such a talent
reed of hewe	a bit deaf
at chirche dore	was better than

The wife of Bathe

W
p.198

A good WIF was <u>ther</u> of <u>biside</u> BATHE,
But she was somdel <u>deef</u>, and that was scathe.
Of <u>clooth-makyng</u> she <u>hadde</u> swich an haunt,
She passed hem of Ypres and of Gaunt …
5 Hir <u>coverchiefs</u> ful fyne weren of ground;
I dorste <u>swere</u> they <u>weyeden</u> ten pound
That on a <u>Sonday</u> weren upon hir <u>heed</u>.
Hir hosen weren of <u>fyn</u> scarlet <u>reed</u>,
Ful streite <u>yteyd</u>, and shoes ful moyste and <u>newe</u>.
10 Boold was <u>hir</u> face, and fair, and <u>reed</u> of hewe.
She was a worthy <u>womman</u> al hir <u>lyve</u>:
<u>Housbondes</u> at <u>chirche</u> dore she hadde <u>fyve</u>, …

*from **The Canterbury Tales General Prologue**
by Geoffrey Chaucer*

Activity 3 ICT WS

1 Re-read the extract opposite aloud. Can you work out the meaning of the words that are underlined? Record them in a table like the one below.

Middle English	Modern English
ther	there
biside	beside

2 Can you identify the word that comes from the old French word *moiste*, meaning wet?

To understand the passage better, it helps to change it into modern English. Start by looking at each word to get a rough idea of the meaning, for example:

> Hir hosen weren of fyn scarlet reed,
> Her stockings were of <u>fine scarlet red</u>,

> Ful streite yteyd, and shoes ful moyste and newe.
> <u>Full straight tied</u> and shoes <u>full moist</u> and new.

This is clearer but it is still not modern English. The underlined words still sound old-fashioned and stilted. Think about how it might be written in modern English: *Her stockings were a lovely scarlet and tightly fastened, and her shoes were soft and new.*

Activity 4 WS

Rewrite the following lines in modern English:

> A good WIF was ther of biside BATHE,
> But she was somdel deef, and that was scathe.
> Of clooth-makyng she hadde swich an haunt,
> She passed hem of Ypres and of Gaunt …

To do this you will need to:

◆ get a rough idea of what each word means
◆ rewrite it in a way that it might be written today.

Remember to use the footnotes opposite to help you.

Activity 5 ⓦⓢ

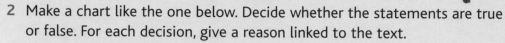

Chaucer describes his characters in detail.
Re-read the description of the Wife of Bath and look at the picture.

1 List the different things you are told about her appearance.

2 Make a chart like the one below. Decide whether the statements are true or false. For each decision, give a reason linked to the text.

Statement	True/False	Reason
She was interested in clothes.	True	Clothes all top quality and expensive.
She was confident.		
She didn't like to be noticed.		
She had very little money.		
She was richly dressed.		
She wanted to be the centre of attention.		
She didn't care about how she looked.		
She was attractive to men.		

Early modern English

In 1476 William Caxton set up his printing press in London. This led to a more standard form of the English language, which was more like English today. Even so, it still needs an extra effort to understand it.

William Shakespeare (1564–1616) is the most famous writer of this early modern period. One of the reasons Shakespeare is so popular is because he uses a wide range of words. Opposite are some examples of the insults he made up. Some of these words may be difficult for you to understand because:

◆ you have not learned the word yet, for example a *caluminous* person is one who spreads lies

◆ the word is archaic and belongs to an earlier time, for example *knave* means 'a dishonest man'.

When you come across words that are difficult to understand you can:

◆ use a dictionary to help you find their meanings

◆ look at what comes before and after to help you guess their meanings.

Try saying some of these insults aloud to a partner. Vary the tone of your voice to suit the insult. You could start your insult with: *Thou art a ...* or *Thou art the ...* (You are ...) or *Get thee gone thou ...* (Go away you ...).

Insults about knaves

p.200

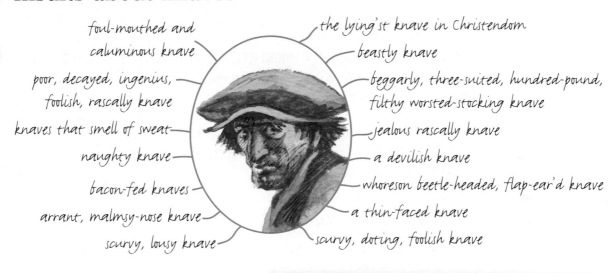

foul-mouthed and caluminous knave

poor, decayed, ingenius, foolish, rascally knave

knaves that smell of sweat

naughty knave

bacon-fed knaves

arrant, malmsy-nose knave

scurvy, lousy knave

the lying'st knave in Christendom

beastly knave

beggarly, three-suited, hundred-pound, filthy worsted-stocking knave

jealous rascally knave

a devilish knave

whoreson beetle-headed, flap-ear'd knave

a thin-faced knave

scurvy, doting, foolish knave

*from **Shukespeare's Insults** by W. F. Hall and G. F. Ötchen*

Word bank

knave – an old word meaning a dishonest man

Activity 6 ⓦⓢ

1 Many of Shakespeare's insults can be grouped under headings, as listed in the chart below. Copy the chart.

Insults about clothes	Insults about smell	Insults about looks	Insults about behaviour

Decide which heading the insults above would come under. Some insults may appear under more than one heading.

2 Make up at least five insults of your own. Follow these rules.

◆ Choose a famous person to insult, such as a pop star or a footballer.

◆ Do not use well-known insults or swear words.

◆ Aim, like Shakespeare, to use a wide range of words.

◆ Make the insults as original and insulting as possible.

You could try to make them sound Shakespearian by starting with *Thou art ...*

Modern English

By the nineteenth century, written English was even closer to what we use today. Charles Dickens was one of the most famous writers of this time. His sentences were often long and complex. You need to be able to break down these long sentences.

Activity 7 ICT WS

Read the extract below. It is the first sentence of one of Dickens's novels, *Our Mutual Friend*, but the order of the clauses has been mixed up.

> **a** between Southwark Bridge which is of iron,
> **b** a boat of dirty and disreputable appearance,
> **c** as an autumn evening was closing in.
> **d** with two figures in it,
> **e** In these times of ours,
> **f** though concerning the exact year there is no need to be precise,
> **g** floated on the Thames,
> **h** and London Bridge which is of stone,

1   With a partner, work out the correct order of the clauses and write out the complete sentence. It will help if you look for:

   ◆ a clause that starts with a capital letter
   ◆ a clause that ends with a full stop
   ◆ any clauses that must come before or after each other.

2   Check your answer with others in your group. Is there anything you need to change?

Now read the next paragraph.

On the look out

The figures in this boat were those of a strong man with ragged **grizzled** hair and a sun-browned face, and a dark girl of nineteen or twenty, recognizable as his daughter. The girl rowed easily; the man, with **rudder-lines** slack in his hands, and his hands loose in his waistband, kept an eager
5   look out. He had no net, hook, or line, and he could not be a fisherman; his boat had no cushion for a sitter, no paint, no inscription, no appliance beyond a rusty boathook and

a coil of rope, and he could not be a waterman; his boat was too crazy and too small to take in cargo for delivery, and he could not be a lighterman or river-
10 carrier; there was no clue to what he looked for, but he looked for something, with a most intent and searching gaze. His daughter watched his face as **earnestly** as he watched the river. But, in the **intensity** of her look there was a touch of dread or horror.

adapted from ***Our Mutual Friend***
by Charles Dickens

Word bank

grizzled – grey, or streaked with grey
rudder-lines – ropes used to steer a boat
earnestly – intently
intensity – strong emotion

Activity 8

Think about the details in the paragraph 'On the look out' that help you to know it was not written this century, or even last century.

1 The man has 'a sun-browned face'. What different words would you use today?

2 Read lines 5 to 10. We are told that the man 'could not be a fisherman'. What other jobs are mentioned? What are you told about them? What do you think they were? Why do we not have these jobs today?

3 List any other clues that show this extract was written over a hundred years ago.

Activity 9

Like many modern writers, Dickens often gave his stories a dramatic start. In the opening of *Our Mutual Friend* he uses words to create a sense of mystery and danger.

1 To help you identify how Dickens does this, sort the phrases below into order by numbering them 1 to 9, where 1 is the phrase that creates *most* sense of mystery and danger, and 9 is the phrase that creates *least* sense of mystery and danger.

> between Southwark Bridge … and London Bridge
> an autumn evening was closing in
> a boat of dirty and disreputable appearance
> ragged grizzled hair
> kept an eager look out
> there was no clue to what he looked for
> a most intent and searching gaze
> the intensity of her look
> a touch of dread or horror

2 Now look at the phrases you have numbered 1 to 4, and underline the words that help to create a sense of mystery and danger.

British and American English

The English language is used in many places across the world. Each place has developed its own vocabulary. There are many differences between British English and American English as you can see in the following passage.

American name for sports shoes.

'I was walking home and the sneakers fell from the sky,' he had told the judge. 'One hit me on the head.'

It had hurt, too.

They hadn't exactly fallen from the sky. He had just walked out from under a freeway overpass when the shoe hit him on the head....

American name for a major road.

Naturally, he had no way of knowing they belonged to Clyde Livingston. In fact, the shoes were anything but sweet. Whoever had worn them had had a bad case of foot odor.

American spelling for 'odour'.

*from **Holes** by Louis Sachar*

Activity 10 ICT WS

The following list contains pairs of words with the same meaning, one the British English word, the other the American English word.

◆ fall	◆ break	◆ rubbish	◆ Maths	◆ autumn	◆ jam
◆ rubber	◆ chips	◆ garbage	◆ jelly	◆ cookie	◆ freeway
◆ favour	◆ recess	◆ Math	◆ vacation	◆ nappy	◆ gasoline
◆ holiday	◆ crisps	◆ sidewalk	◆ trousers	◆ chemists	◆ biscuit
◆ trainers	◆ pavement	◆ drugstore	◆ motorway	◆ pants	◆ diaper
◆ eraser	◆ favor	◆ petrol	◆ allowance	◆ pocket money	

1   Using a chart like the one below, sort the words into British English and American English.

2   As you do this, make a note of how you worked out the meaning of the American word. Was it through:

   ◆ clues in the words?   ◆ your knowledge of word families?   ◆ TV?

British English	American English	How I knew
autumn	fall	Clue in the word – autumn is the time when leaves fall from the trees

English and the computer age

One of the most rapid changes in the English language has been brought about by the computer age. Words such as 'CD-ROM' and 'byte' are now part of the language.

Electronic messages (e-messages) and electronic mail (e-mail) are both ways of exchanging messages online. In e-messages, both the sender and the receiver are logged on to their computers at the same time; in e-mails, a message is left in a 'mail box' for later reading. The style of e-messages and e-mails is often more like spoken English than written letters. A whole new set of rules is developing around these messages.

Activity 11 ICT WS

Read the following e-mails between two friends:

W
p.198

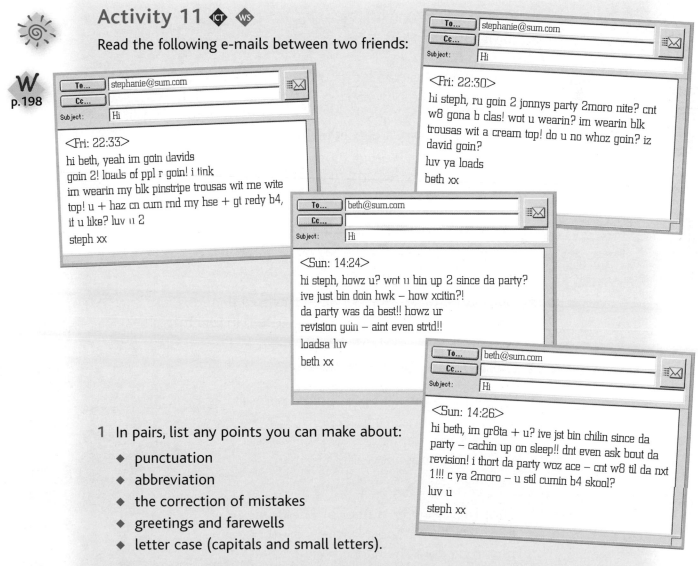

To... stephanie@sum.com
Cc...
Subject: Hi

<Fri: 22:33>
hi beth, yeah im goin davids
goin 2! loads of ppl r goin! i tink
im wearin my blk pinstripe trousas wit me wite
top! u + haz cn cum rnd my hse + gt redy b4,
if u like? luv u 2
steph xx

To... stephanie@sum.com
Cc...
Subject: Hi

<Fri: 22:30>
hi steph, ru goin 2 jonnys party 2moro nite? cnt
w8 gona b clas! wot u wearin? im wearin blk
trousas wit a cream top! do u no whoz goin? iz
david goin?
luv ya loads
beth xx

To... beth@sum.com
Cc...
Subject: Hi

<Sun: 14:24>
hi steph, howz u? wot u bin up 2 since da party?
ive just bin doin hwk – how xcitin?!
da party was da best!! howz ur
revision goin – aint even strtd!!
loadsa luv
beth xx

To... beth@sum.com
Cc...
Subject: Hi

<Sun: 14:26>
hi beth, im gr8ta + u? ive jst bin chilin since da
party – cachin up on sleep!! dnt even ask bout da
revision! i thort da party woz ace – cnt w8 til da nxt
1!!! c ya 2moro – u stil cumin b4 skool?
luv u
steph xx

1 In pairs, list any points you can make about:

   ◆ punctuation

   ◆ abbreviation

   ◆ the correction of mistakes

   ◆ greetings and farewells

   ◆ letter case (capitals and small letters).

2 Why do you think e-mails are written in this way? List at least three reasons.

3 Using your answers to 1 and 2, produce five clear instructions on how you might write an informal e-mail to a friend.

English across time

Activity 12 WS

Below is a timeline, showing the history of the British Isles from 500 AD to the present day. Look back through this unit to help you decide where the different events, labelled a–j below, should be placed along the timeline. Copy the timeline. Add the events and the dates, where appropriate, in the correct positions.

a Invention of e-mail.

b More than 10,000 French words came into the English language.

c The English lost the Battle of Hastings to the Normans.

d William Shakespeare, possibly the most famous playwright of all times, wrote in Early Modern English: 'arrant, malmsy-nose knave'.

e Charles Dickens, author of *Our Mutual Friend*, wrote in Modern English: 'there was no clue to what he looked for, but he looked for something with intent and searching gaze'.

f The Battle of Maldon between the English and the Vikings gave rise to a poem, written in Old English.

g Invention of the first computer.

h William Caxton set up his printing press.

i The Saxons, the Angles and the Jutes, all from the most powerful German nations, start to invade Britain.

j Geoffrey Chaucer, author of *The Canterbury Tales*, wrote in Middle English: 'Husbondes at chirche dore she hadde fyve'.

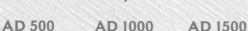

AD 500   AD 1000   AD 1500   AD 2000

This unit will help you to:

◆ understand and interpret the detail of a text

◆ use detail from the text when answering questions

◆ develop your personal response to a text

◆ compare characters within a text.

Understanding detail

It is important to understand the detail of a text so that you can work out what is happening. Read this short story carefully, answering the questions that follow.

The Breadwinner

The parents of a boy of fourteen were waiting for him to come home with his first week's wages.

The mother had laid the table and was cutting some slices of bread and butter for tea. She was a little woman with a pinched face and a **spare** body,
5   dressed in a blue blouse and skirt, the front of the skirt covered with a starched white apron. She looked tired and frequently sighed heavily.

The father, sprawling inelegantly in an old armchair by the fireside, legs outstretched, was little too. He had watery blue eyes and a heavy brown moustache, which he sucked occasionally.
10   These people were plainly poor, for the room, though clean, was **meanly** furnished, and the thick pieces of bread and butter were the only food on the table.

What have you learned so far about:

◆ the mother?   ◆ the father?   ◆ their home?

As she prepared the meal, the woman from time to time looked **contemptuously** at her husband. He ignored her, raising his eyebrows, humming, or tapping his teeth now and then with his finger-nails, making a pretence of being **profoundly** bored.

15 'You'll keep your hands off the money,' said the woman, obviously repeating something that she had already said several times before. 'I know what'll happen to it if you get hold of it. He'll give it to me. It'll pay the rent and buy us a bit of food, and not go into the till at the nearest public-house.'

'You shut your mouth,' said the man, quietly.

20 'I'll not shut my mouth!' cried the woman, in a quick burst of anger. 'Why should I shut my mouth? You've been boss here for long enough. I put up with it when you were bringing money into the house, but I'll not put up with it now. You're nobody here. Understand? *Nobody. I'm* boss and he'll hand the money to me!'

'We'll see about that,' said the man, leisurely poking the fire.

25 Nothing more was said for about five minutes.

What are the mother and father arguing about?

Then the boy came in. He did not look older than ten or eleven years. He looked absurd in long trousers. The whites of his eyes against his black face gave him a startled expression.

The father got to his feet.

30 'Where's the money?' he demanded.

The boy looked from one to the other. He was afraid of his father. He licked his pale lips.

'Come on now,' said the man. 'Where's the money?'

'Don't give it to him,' said the woman. 'Don't give it to him, Billy. Give it to me.'

35 The father advanced on the boy, his teeth showing in a snarl under his big moustache.

'Where's the money?' he almost whispered.

The boy looked him straight in the eyes.

'I lost it,' he said.

40 'You – *what*?' cried his father.

'I lost it,' the boy repeated.

The man began to shout and wave his hands about.

'Lost it! *Lost* it! What are you talking about? How could you lose it?'

'It was in a packet,' said the boy, 'a little envelope. I lost it.'

45 'Where did you lose it?'

'I don't know. I must have dropped it in the street.'

'Did you go back and look for it?'

The boy nodded. 'I couldn't find it,' he said.

> ## Word bank
> **spare** – thin or lean
> **meanly** – poorly, not generously
> **contemptuously** – with scorn
> **profoundly** – extremely

Why is the boy in trouble?

The man made a noise in his throat, half grunt, half moan – the sort of noise that an
50 animal would make.

'So you lost it, did you?' he said. He stepped back a couple of paces and took off
his belt – a wide, thick belt with a heavy brass buckle. 'Come here,' he said.

The boy, biting his lower lip so as to keep back the tears, advanced, and the man
raised his arm. The woman, motionless until that moment, leapt forward and seized
55 it. Her husband, finding strength in his blind rage, pushed her aside easily. He
brought the belt down on the boy's back. He beat him unmercifully about the body
and legs. The boy sank to the floor, but did not cry out.

When the man had spent himself, he put on the belt and pulled the boy to his feet.
'Now you'll get off to bed,' he said.

60 'The lad wants some food,' said the woman.

'He'll go to bed. Go and wash yourself.'

Without a word the boy went into the **scullery** and washed his hands and face.
When he had done this he went straight upstairs.

What does the father do?   What does the mother do?

The man sat down at the table, ate some bread and butter and drank two cups of
65 tea. The woman ate nothing. She sat opposite him, never taking her eyes from his
face, looking with hatred at him. Just as before, he took no notice of her, ignored
her, behaved as if she were not there at all.

When he had finished the meal he went out.

Immediately he had shut the door the woman jumped to her feet and ran
70 upstairs to the boy's room.

He was sobbing bitterly, his face buried in the pillow. She sat on the edge of the
bed and put her arms about him, pressed him close to her breast, ran her fingers
through his disordered hair, whispered **endearments**, **consoling** him. He let her do
this, finding comfort in her caresses, relief in his own tears.

75 After a while his weeping ceased. He raised his head and smiled at her, his
wet eyes bright. Then he put his hand under the pillow and withdrew a small
dirty envelope.

'Here's the money,' he whispered.

She took the envelope and opened it
80 and pulled out a long strip of paper with
some figures on it – **a ten shilling note**
and a **sixpence**.

*from **The Breadwinner** by Leslie Howard*

How does the mother comfort her son?
What had happened to the money?

Word bank

scullery – back kitchen
endearments – words of affection
consoling – comforting
ten shilling note – old money,
equal to about 50 pence
sixpence – old money, equal to
about 2 ½ pence

Interpreting detail

Once you have *understood* the detail of a story, you can use it to develop your own ideas. When you do this you are *interpreting* the detail. Think about this exam question:

What do you learn about the mother from lines 1 to 6 ('The parents … sighed heavily.')?

Activity 1 WS

Step 1: First re-read lines 1 to 6. This is the information you are given about the mother. Highlight the details that seem important, as shown below.

> She was a little woman with a <u>pinched face and a spare body</u>, dressed in a blue blouse and skirt, the front of the skirt <u>covered with a starched white apron</u>. She looked <u>tired and frequently sighed heavily</u>.

Step 2: Then ask questions. Why has the writer used words such as 'pinched' and 'sighed'? What is the importance of the 'starched white apron'? What is the writer trying to tell the reader about the mother? Match the details to what they suggest.

Details	Interpretation
a pinched face and spare body	she kept herself clean and tidy
a starched white apron	she was unhappy
she frequently sighed heavily	she was unwell and/or underfed

Step 3: Finally, answer the question 'What do you learn about the mother from lines 1 to 6?' by putting the details together with what they tell you. The following answer is annotated to show you a student's thoughts as he wrote:

The story tells me she is 'little'. I use my own word 'small' for my explanation.

For variety, I give my evidence first in this sentence. I introduce the evidence with the word 'as' and use 'it suggests' to introduce my thoughts on what 'starched' tells me.

> The mother was a small woman. She might not have been very well as she is described as having 'a pinched face and a spare body'. She wore a starched apron over the front of her skirt. As the apron was starched it suggests she took care to stay clean and tidy. She looked tired and sighed heavily, which makes it seem as though she was unhappy or that something was worrying her.

I cannot be sure that she is ill. Therefore, I say 'might'.

Because I'm not sure, I introduce evidence to back up my point. I use the words 'as she is described as' to introduce my evidence.

Instead of saying 'it suggests' again, I decided to use the phrase 'which makes it seem as though'.

Activity 2 ᴡꜱ

Copy and complete the chart below. The first column gives you details from the text that begins on page 19. Find these details. In the second column write what you have learned from reading these details. The first one is done for you.

Details	Interpretation
It'll pay the rent and buy us a bit of food, and not go into the till at the nearest public-house.	This suggests that they do not have very much money and that the father spends what they do have at the pub.
I put up with it when you were bringing money into the house …	This makes me think that …
The boy looked him straight in the eyes.	The fact the boy does this shows that …
The boy sank to the floor, but did not cry out.	The boy's actions show that …
Immediately he had shut the door the woman jumped to her feet and ran upstairs to the boy's room.	This gives the impression that …
'Here's the money,' he whispered.	This suggests that …

Using details from the text to answer a question

When you are answering questions about a text, it is important to use details from the text as evidence to back up your comments. This shows your examiner that you have thought about the text and can support your point of view. You can:

◆ use a particular detail from the text, for example:

Comment	Evidence
It sounds as though the father drinks a lot.	The mother wants the money to buy food and pay the rent. She is afraid that if the father gets it he will spend it on drink.

◆ use a quotation, for example:

Comment	Evidence
It sounds as though the father drinks a lot.	The mother wants the money to buy food and pay the rent. She is afraid that if the father gets it, it will go 'into the till at the nearest public-house'.

Activity 3 ⓦⓢ

1 Copy and complete the chart below by finding an appropriate detail or quotation to support the comments about the boy. The first one has been done for you.

Comment on the boy	Evidence
He looked younger than his age.	We are told that the boy was fourteen but that 'He did not look older than ten or eleven years'.
He shows courage when dealing with his father.	
He refuses to give in to his father.	
He is very upset by what has happened.	
He cares about his mother.	

2 Use the information from your chart to write a paragraph explaining what you learn about the boy from the story. Remember to give your supporting evidence.

Developing your personal response to a text

The story of *The Breadwinner* will affect different readers in different ways, depending on their backgrounds and life experiences. You need to be able to work out how *you* are affected by the story and why. This is called your **personal response**.

A question that targets personal response is:

> *What do you think of the way the father behaves in this story?*

This question is about two things:

◆ the way the father behaves
◆ your thoughts on this.

To answer this you need to spend time thinking about the father.

Activity 4

Think carefully about the father's behaviour.

Step 1: Make notes on how the father behaves towards his wife and son. Read the text for evidence. These are the kinds of notes you could make:

Father to wife:	Talks to her nastily — 'You shut your mouth' (l. 19)
	Violent to her — pushes her to one side (l. 55)
	Acts as though she's not there (l. 66 and 67)
Father to son:	Expects him to hand over the money (l. 30)
	Tries to frighten him — his teeth showing in a snarl (l. 35 and 36)
	Very violent towards him — beats him with a buckled belt (l. 52)

Step 2: Now talk about the following questions with a partner and make short notes on your answers.

1 Why does the father behave in this way? Can you find any clues in the text? You will need to look for hidden meaning or read between the lines.

2 Do you know anyone like the father? Think about people you know personally and also characters on television or in books.

3 What do you think about his actions?

4 How do his actions make you feel? Why do they make you feel like this?

Think over what you have discussed. Are there any questions on which you and your partner have different opinions? What are the reasons for the difference?

Only when you have explored a range of questions about the father's behaviour and your response to it are you ready to answer the main question in Activity 5.

Activity 5 ICT

Now you need to plan and write your answer to the question:

What do you think of the way the father behaves in this story?

To answer it fully you need to write about:

◆ how the father behaves towards the mother and the son
◆ what you think about this.

Use your notes from Activity 4 to help you. It may also help you to organise your answer in this way.

Paragraph 1: Describe how the father behaves towards the mother. Comment on his behaviour and use evidence from the text to support your points.

Paragraph 2: Describe how the father behaves towards his son. Comment on his behaviour and use evidence from the text to support the points you make.

Paragraph 3: Explain how you think and feel about the father's behaviour. Give your reasons for your thoughts and feelings.

Remember to write in a formal style. You could use the following words and phrases in your answer.

◆ as, so, because, therefore	◆ implying that, possibly
◆ it would seem that	◆ this gives an impression of
◆ this suggests that	◆ however, possibly

When you have finished, check that you have developed your ideas and referred to the text by:

◆ numbering the different points you have made (if you have made the same point twice you need to cross one out)
◆ underlining all references to the text (if you have made a point without giving evidence, add the evidence).

Comparing characters in a text

When you compare characters you look for similarities and differences between them.

You are going to compare the mother and the father in *The Breadwinner*. Start by thinking about each of them separately.

The mother in *The Breadwinner*

> *She was a little woman with a pinched face and a spare body, dressed in a blue blouse and skirt, the front of the skirt covered with a starched white apron. She looked tired and frequently sighed heavily.*

She thinks her husband will spend the money on drink.
She has no respect for her husband.
She tries to defend her son by leaping forward and seizing the belt.
After the beating she looks with hatred at her husband.
She is close to her son and physically comforts him.
She lets her son suffer in order to get the money.

The father in *The Breadwinner*

> *The father, sprawling inelegantly in an old armchair by the fireside, legs outstretched, was little too. He had watery blue eyes and a heavy brown moustache, which he sucked occasionally.*

He ignores his wife.
He spends the housekeeping money at the pub.
His son is afraid of him.
He is furious when his son says he's lost the money.
He beats his son with a wide, thick belt with a heavy brass buckle.
After the beating he behaves as though his wife isn't there.

Activity 6 ⓦⓢ

You worked out how you felt about the father in Activity 4. Now work out how you feel about the mother. Talk about and make notes on the following questions.

1 How do you think the mother feels about her husband and her son?

2 Do you think she was right to act as she did? What else could she have done?

3 How do you feel about her? Explain why you feel as you do.

4 Do you know anyone like the mother? Think about the people you know personally and characters on television or in books.

Activity 7

Now you are ready to put all the pieces together. Look back over your work in Activities 4, 5 and 6 and your notes on the mother and the father to help you answer the following question:

> *Compare the mother with the father in* The Breadwinner. *Explain your thoughts and feelings about them.*

Read all of the following before you start to write.

1 Here are some ideas for how you could organise your writing.

> **Step 1** Write about the appearance of the father and the mother.
>
> **Step 2** Write about how they behave towards each other.
>
> **Step 3** Describe what each one wants to do with the money.
>
> **Step 4** Describe how the father behaves towards his son.
>
> **Step 5** Describe how the mother behaves towards the son.
>
> **Step 6** Explain how you feel about the father and why.
>
> **Step 7** Explain how you feel about the mother and why.

2 As you are writing remember to:

- ◆ point out similarities or differences between the mother and the father
- ◆ give evidence to support what you say
- ◆ write mainly in the present tense
- ◆ write in standard English.

3 Here are some words and phrases that will help you to link your ideas.

> - ◆ They are similar (different) in that they …
> - ◆ whereas …   ◆ Similarly …
> - ◆ In both cases …   ◆ I can tell this by …
> - ◆ This is evident when …   ◆ Both the mother and the father …

Activity 8

1 When you have finished writing, assess your own work by highlighting or labelling:

- ◆ the points of similarity and difference you have made
- ◆ the different pieces of evidence you have used
- ◆ the places where you have developed your personal viewpoint.

2 Award your work a mark from a range of 1 to 10. Give three clear reasons for the mark you have awarded. State one area where you could improve your work.

This unit will help you to:

◆ identify the writer's voice
◆ think about the ways the writer presents ideas
◆ think about how the writer explores attitudes and issues.

Identifying the voice

How much do you learn about a writer from his or her writing? Talk about the following statements. Do you agree with them? Do they match different things you have read?

> He said it, so he must believe it.

> Writers sometimes use characters to make their points for them.

> A writer's work often reveals his or her cultural background.

> A writer sometimes disagrees with his characters – that's the whole point!

> Just because it's written down doesn't mean it's true.

> A writer creates a world – he doesn't have to believe in it.

> You can tell it's not an English writer because of the way it's written.

> If a writer uses the first person, then he or she is speaking directly to the reader.

> Writers don't always say what they mean or mean what they say.

As you may have realised from your discussion, a writer will not always speak directly to the reader, even when he or she uses the first person.

Activity 1

As you read the poem below:

◆ list the clues that help you identify the owner of the voice
◆ note the point at which you identified with certainty the owner of the voice.

The Caged Bird in Springtime

What can it be,
This curious anxiety?
It is as if I wanted
To fly away from here.

5 But how absurd!
I have never flown in my life,
And I do not know
What flying means, though I have heard,
Of course, something about it.

10 Why do I peck the wires of this little cage?
It is the only nest I have ever known.
But I want to build my own,
High in the secret branches of the air.

I cannot quite remember how
15 It is done, but I know
That what I want to do
Cannot be done here.

I have all I need –
Seed and water, air and light.
20 Why, then, do I weep with anguish,
And beat my head and my wings
Against those sharp wires, while the children
Smile at each other, saying: 'Hark how he sings?'

James Kirkup

Activity 2 ICT WS

1 From the poem, identify:

- ◆ what the bird's life is like
- ◆ what the bird feels that it wants to do.

2 The writer sometimes shows us the bird's feelings indirectly.

> Why do I peck the wires of this little cage?

Tells the reader indirectly that the bird feels trapped in a small place.

Look at the following examples. What do the underlined words tell you indirectly about how the bird really feels?

> High in the <u>secret</u> branches of the air.
> Against those <u>sharp</u> wires,

3 Re-read the last four lines of the poem. What misunderstanding is shown here? Why do you think the poet chose to end the poem in this way?

4 As we look in detail at a poem, we often find that it can be interpreted in more than one way. Think about 'The Caged Bird in Springtime'.

- ◆ Does this poem have to be about a bird?
- ◆ Is there any way it could be about a person?
- ◆ Could it be about a teacher or a parent, for example?
- ◆ Could it be about someone who lives in a city or in the countryside?
- ◆ Could it be about someone like you?

5 The poem could be about a student in school. Re-read the poem with a partner and talk about what each line would mean for a student who wanted to escape from school. The first stanza has been done for you:

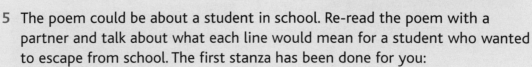

What can it be, This curious anxiety? It is as if I wanted To fly away from here.	*Why am I feeling so fed-up and worried? It's as though I could just get up and walk out.*

Looking for clues

Sometimes a writer will seem to speak directly to the reader and the poem will be based on personal experience. The reader can often tell when this is happening because there are clues in the text.

Activity 3

Read the poem 'A Constable Calls' carefully two or three times (see opposite). Then, using a chart like the one below, place the following events in the order in which they are described. The first event is 'e'.

a Speaker wonders if father is telling truth about crops.

b Constable looks at speaker as he says goodbye.

c Constable unstraps heavy ledger.

d Speaker stares at constable's gun holster.

e Constable parks bicycle by window-sill.

f Speaker hears sound of bicycle ticking.

g Speaker feels guilty and imagines punishment place in barracks.

h Constable sits, placing hat by side of chair.

i Constable closes the domesday book.

j Speaker's father working out tillage returns.

1	2	3	4	5	6	7	8	9	10
e									

You can check your answers at the end of this unit.

A Constable Calls

His bicycle stood at the window-sill,
The rubber **cowl** of a mud-splasher
Skirting the front mudguard,
Its fat black handlegrips

5　Heating in sunlight, the 'spud'
Of the **dynamo** gleaming and cocked back,
The pedal treads hanging relieved
Of the boot of the law.

His cap was upside down
10　On the floor, next his chair.
The line of its pressure ran like a **bevel**
In his slightly sweating hair.

He had unstrapped
The heavy **ledger**, and my father
15　Was making **tillage** returns
In **acres, roods, and perches**.

Arithmetic and fear.
I sat staring at the polished holster
With its buttoned flap, the braid cord
20　Looped into the revolver butt.

'Any other root crops?
Mangolds? Marrowstems? Anything like that?'
'No.' But was there not a line
Of turnips where the seed ran out

25　In the potato field? I assumed
Small guilts and sat
Imagining the black hole in the barracks.
He stood up, shifted the **baton**-case

Further round on his belt,
30　Closed **the domesday book**,
Fitted his cap back with two hands,
And looked at me as he said goodbye.

A shadow bobbed in the window.
He was snapping the carrier spring
35　Over the ledger. His boot pushed off
And the bicycle ticked, ticked, ticked.

Seamus Heaney

Word bank

cowl – a monk's hood; cover
dynamo – energy converter
bevel – sloping edge
ledger – a book for recording details
tillage – produce of the land
acres, roods, and perches –
different measurements of area
and length
baton – long wooden stick or old-
fashioned truncheon
the domesday book – the original
Domesday or Doomsday Book was a
survey of the land of England in 1086

Activity 4 ⓦⓢ

1 The poem tells of a visit by a constable (policeman). Do you think it is based on something that once happened to the poet? Copy the chart below and make notes on the details given about the memory to help you decide. Notes about the policeman's bicycle have been done for you.

The memory	Details relating to the memory
The policeman's bicycle	Rubber cowl, mud-splasher, fat black handlegrips, spud of the dynamo gleaming, pedal treads hanging relieved, the bicycle ticked, ticked, ticked
The policeman – clothing – physical appearance – items he carries	
The policeman's actions	
The father's actions/words	
The son's feelings	

If you have a photocopy of the poem you could highlight and annotate the details, rather than making separate notes.

2 Talk with a partner about whether Heaney is speaking directly to the reader about something that once happened to him. Give reasons based on your notes.

Thinking about the cultural context

Sometimes it helps our understanding of a poem to have some awareness of the cultural context in which it was written. Seamus Heaney, who wrote 'A Constable Calls', is an Irish poet. He was raised as a Roman Catholic and lived on his father's small farm in Northern Ireland where there was conflict and suspicion between the Roman Catholic and Protestant communities. The constable would have been a Protestant.

Activity 5 ICT

Re-read 'A Constable Calls' closely. The knowledge of the conflict between the Roman Catholic and Protestant communities can help you to understand the poem better. Using a chart like the one below, match the following features (1–6) from the poem with the explanations of them (a–f) (the first one has been done for you).

1 The way Heaney describes the constable, for example 'the boot of the law' (line 8).
2 Heaney's fascination with the gun.
3 The father's single-word reply (line 23).
4 Heaney's feelings of guilt.
5 The mention of the black hole in the barracks (line 27).
6 The final line of the poem.

   a This was probably a place to be feared, where offenders were placed.
   b The tick, tick, tick is like a bomb about to explode.
   c Heaney would know of people who had been killed by guns.
   d This makes you think of violence, like 'putting the boot in'.
   e Heaney is afraid they are going to get into trouble.
   f The father is being deliberately unhelpful and unfriendly.

1	2	3	4	5	6
d					

Looking at features of style

One quality of Heaney's poetry is the way he uses pauses and the sounds of words for effect. Here are some features of 'A Constable Calls':

PAUSES
When a line of poetry has a strong pause at the end it is called **end-stopped**. This is sometimes marked by punctuation. For example:

His bicycle stood at the window-sill, (line 1)

When a line of poetry moves on to the next line with almost no pause it is called **run-on**. For example:

The rubber cowl of a mud-splasher
Skirting the front mudguard (lines 2 and 3)

The effect of this run-on line is called **enjambment**.

Heaney's use of end-stopped and run-on lines has a direct effect on the way the poem is read aloud. In pairs, re-read the poem aloud, taking particular notice of end-stopped and run-on lines.

SOUNDS: CONSONANCE

Repetition of sound is used to produce echoes within and between lines. Where there is repetition of consonant sounds it is called **consonance**. For example:

the black hole in the barracks (line 27)

Here the repetition of the 'b' and 'ck' sounds reinforces a sense of the harshness of the imagined place.

Find and copy one other example of consonance in the poem. Try to explain why Heaney has used sound in this way.

SOUNDS: ASSONANCE

Where there is repetition of vowel sounds it is called **assonance**. For example:

Its fat black handlegrips (line 4)

The short vowel sound is harsh. Here the repetition of the 'a' sound links the three words and gives a sense of unpleasantness.

Find and copy one other example of assonance in the poem. Try to explain why Heaney has used sound in this way.

Exploring attitudes and issues

People sometimes have fixed views about other groups of people. They don't see them as individuals. They expect them all to dress, act and think in a certain way.

The businessman
◆ Goes to work on the train
◆ Wears a pinstriped suit and a bowler hat
◆ Carries a briefcase and an umbrella
◆ Reads *The Times* newspaper

The builder
◆ Avoids work
◆ Overweight and smokes
◆ Whistles at girls
◆ Reads tabloid newspapers

Grouping people together in this way is called **stereotyping**.

Activity 6

In pairs, list the different things you link with these stereotypes.

> ◆ the football fan ◆ the model ◆ the teenager

If you are good at drawing, you could quickly sketch and annotate one of them.

Sometimes people stereotype people from other countries. John Agard was born in Guyana, on the north-east coast of South America, when it was still a British colony. He moved to England in 1977 when he was 28. The West Indian culture plays an important part in what and how he writes. In his poem 'Stereotype' he deliberately uses the voice of the West Indian stereotype.

Activity 7

1 Before reading the poem, work in pairs to chart what you already know about West Indian culture. It might help you to think about the following.

> ◆ place names ◆ types of food ◆ carnivals ◆ traditions
> ◆ famous people ◆ religion ◆ types of music

2 Now read the poem on page 38 through once carefully. As you read, list all the words and phrases that are linked with the West Indian stereotype.

Stereotype

I'm a fullblooded
West Indian stereotype
See me straw hat?
Watch it good

5 I'm a fullblooded
West Indian stereotype
You ask
if I got riddum
in me blood
10 You going ask!
Man just beat de drum
and don't forget
to pour de rum

I'm a fullblooded
15 West Indian stereotype
You say
I suppose you can show
us the **limbo**, can't you?
How you know!
20 How you know!
You sure
you don't want me
sing you a **calypso** too
How about that

25 I'm a fullblooded
West Indian stereotype
You call me
happy-go-lucky
Yes that's me
30 dressing fancy
and chasing woman
if you think ah lie
bring yuh sister

I'm a fullblooded
35 West Indian stereotype
You wonder
where do you people
get such riddum
could it be the sunshine
40 My goodness
just listen to that steelband

Isn't there one thing
you forgot to ask
go on man ask ask
45 This native will answer anything
How about cricket?
I suppose you're good at it?
Hear this man
good at it!
50 Put de **willow**
in me hand
and watch me strike
de boundary

Yes I'm a fullblooded
55 West Indian stereotype

that's why I
graduated from Oxford University
with a degree
in **anthropology**

John Agard

Word bank

limbo – where the dancer literally bends
over backwards to pass under a bar
calypso – a West Indian song that has a topical meaning
willow – another way of saying 'cricket bat'
anthropology – the study of people and their customs

Activity 8 ICT WS

Agard's poetry is often performed. The sounds of the words and the way they are spoken are very important.

In pairs, you are going to prepare a reading of 'Stereotype'. Follow these steps.

Step 1: Think about the way Agard uses language to create certain effects. You can do this by asking a series of questions. See how this works with the first two stanzas:

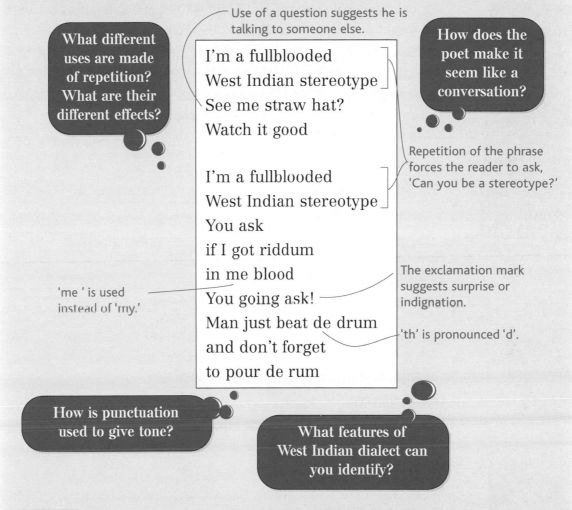

Use of a question suggests he is talking to someone else.

What different uses are made of repetition? What are their different effects?

How does the poet make it seem like a conversation?

I'm a fullblooded
West Indian stereotype
See me straw hat?
Watch it good

I'm a fullblooded
West Indian stereotype
You ask
if I got riddum
in me blood
You going ask!
Man just beat de drum
and don't forget
to pour de rum

Repetition of the phrase forces the reader to ask, 'Can you be a stereotype?'

'me ' is used instead of 'my.'

The exclamation mark suggests surprise or indignation.

'th' is pronounced 'd'.

How is punctuation used to give tone?

What features of West Indian dialect can you identify?

Step 2: Stereotypes don't exist in real life. They are exaggerated images and often not very complimentary. Think about and make notes on the following.

◆ How is the West Indian stereotype made to seem ridiculous?

◆ What is the tone of the stanza? What point is the speaker making?

◆ Why do you think the poet chose to speak through the voice of a stereotype?

Step 3: Re-read the whole poem closely to identify how it should be read aloud. Either make notes or highlight and annotate a photocopy of the poem. Aim to produce a lively and interesting reading of the poem.

Comparing two poems

At first 'A Constable Calls' and 'Stereotype' might seem very different.
On closer reading, however, they do have some similarities.

Activity 9

1 Use the work you have done on both poems to help you complete the chart
below. It will help you to identify similarities and differences between the poems.
Highlight or underline the similarities in one colour and the differences in another.

Area for comparison	'A Constable Calls' by Seamus Heaney	'Stereotype' by John Agard
The poet's cultural background	Roman Catholic – born in Northern Ireland Much suspicion between Catholics and Protestants – constable was Protestant	
Subject of poem		The way West Indians are stereotyped
How the subject is linked to the cultural context	Shows fear, guilt	
Use of rhyme	Only one end-rhyme: 'chair'/'hair' Some internal rhyme, e.g. 'And looked at <u>me</u> as <u>he</u> said goodbye'	
Use of dialect		
How punctuation is used	End-stopped and run-on lines	
How repetition of words and/or sounds is used		
The voice of the poet		First person – uses voice of the stereotype

2 Now you have thought carefully about both poems, decide which one you most
like. Write a short paragraph giving at least three separate reasons for your choice.

Answers for Activity 3, p. 32 as follows:

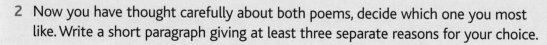

1	2	3	4	5	6	7	8	9	10
e	h	c	j	d	a	g	i	b	f

You are going to compare two poems: 'Dress Sense' by David Kitchen and 'Dread-lock Style' by Lesley Miranda. This assignment will take about one hour.

WS 1 Spend 20 minutes reading the poems on pages 42 and 43 closely, then answer *all* the questions that follow them. List the points you wish to make and the evidence you wish to use, or make notes on a chart like this. You will be awarded marks for your notes.

Points of comparison	'Dress Sense'	'Dread-lock Style'
What the poem is about		
Who the speaker is and what you learn about him/her		
How we are given the impression of someone talking	Asks lots of questions, e.g. 'You're asking me what's wrong with that?' Speaks as though replying, e.g. 'No. I'm not going to explain.' It's as though it's half a conversation.	
Ways the poet uses rhyme and/or repetition		
Ways the poet uses punctuation		Doesn't use much: capitals for 'Me' and 'So' and 'I' – perhaps to emphasise these words. No full stops – maybe to show he's thinking aloud.
What the poet wants the reader to think		
The way the poem makes you think and feel		
Other points		

15 marks

Dress Sense

You're not going out in that, are you?
I've never seen anything
More ridiculous in my whole life.
You look like you've been dragged
5 Through a hedge backwards
And lost half your dress along the way.

What's wrong with it?
You're asking me what's wrong with that?
Everything: that's what.
10 It's loud, it's common,
It **reveals** too much of your …
Your … well your 'what you shouldn't be revealing'.

No. I'm not going to explain:
You know very well what I mean, young lady
15 But you choose to ignore
Every single piece of reasonable helpful advice
That you are offered.

It's not just the neckline I'm talking about
– And you can hardly describe it as a neckline,
20 More like a **navel**-line
If you bother to observe the way that it plunges.
Have you taken a look at the back?
(What little there is of it.)
Have you?

25 Boys are only going to think
One thing
When they see you in that outfit.
Where on earth did you get it?
And don't tell me that my money paid for it
30 Whatever you do.

You found it where?

Well, it probably looked different on her
And, anyway, you shouldn't be going through
Your mother's old clothes.

David Kitchen

Word bank
reveals – shows
navel – belly button

Dread-lock Style

Me don't want no hair style
cause me don't want no hair pile
pon me bedroom floor

I say me don't want no hair style
5 cause me don't want no hair pile
pon me bedroom floor

I think I gonna stick to me
dread-lock style
me dread-lock style
10 looking wild wild wild

dem hair gals
putting a dunno what on yuh hair
bunning up yuh scalp
thinking I was born yesterday

15 So I think I gonna stick
to me dread-lock style
me dread-lock style
looking wild wild wild

Lesley Miranda

2 You now have 40 minutes to write your comparison of 'Dress Sense' and 'Dread-lock Style'.

Use the notes you have made to help you to:

◆ point out similarities and differences between the poems
◆ use evidence from the poems to support the points you make.

Here are some useful words and phrases:

◆ In contrast to …	◆ Whereas …
◆ Similarly …	◆ In both cases …
◆ Both poems …	◆ They are similar (different) in so far as …

Remember to write in:

◆ standard English   ◆ the present tense.

35 marks
TOTAL 50 marks

Section B ◆ Writing to imagine, explore and entertain
Introduction

In the last two years the focus of your work has been on how to develop narratives and how to use language imaginatively for different effects in a range of poetry. You have experimented with figurative language and with different forms. In the units that follow you will explore a range of forms, including non-fiction. It isn't only in fiction and poetry that language can be shaped imaginatively to entertain readers.

In Unit 5, *Crafting stories*, you will explore some of the ways stories can be shaped and how they can be told from different points of view.

In Unit 6, *Writing to entertain*, you will focus on a range of non-fiction writing, including journalism and travel writing. You will look at how writers exploit language to convey and explore ideas in entertaining ways.

In Unit 7, *Developing ideas in different forms*, you will explore a range of poetic forms. You will think about how things like rhyme and rhythm give shape to ideas.

Unit 8 tests you on the skills you will develop as you work carefully through the three units.

This unit will help you to:

◆ explore different kinds of narrative perspective

◆ structure stories in different ways

◆ develop your range of sentence styles and punctuation.

Perspective

Perspective is about **point of view**. Different people see the same thing in different ways because they see it from a different point of view.

Activity 1 ⓌⓈ

1 Look at the four drawings below. Match drawings 2, 3 and 4 with the person whose point of view it is:

◆ robber   ◆ woman   ◆ police officers.

2 The four points of view are very different. Copy and complete the chart below.

Whose point of view?	What would be seen
The 'bird's-eye view'	You can see <u>everything</u> from this point of view.
The robber	The robber would notice the woman but not the police.
The woman	
The police officers	

A narrative perspective is the point of view from which a writer chooses to tell a story. If you were going to write the story of the bank robbery as shown in the pictures above you could tell it from the point of view of the robber, the woman, the two police officers or from a point of view that lets you see everything.

Activity 2 ICT

If you chose to write the story from the point of view of the robber, you might begin:

> The alarm went off before I got any money so I rushed out of the bank. There was a woman right outside on the pavement and I crashed into her.

You use 'I' because you are in the story and you are telling it.

1 How might you begin if:
   a you were the woman?
   b you were one of the police officers?
   c you were going to write from the point of view of a writer who could see everything but was not in the story?

2 In **a** and **b** you will have used the pronouns 'I' and 'we'. Which pronouns do you use in **c**?

These different points of view are described in the following ways.

1 **First person**: the story is told from the point of view of one of the characters in it. This character is identified as: **I** (first person singular) or **we** (first person plural). For example:

> My footprints track across the faint dew still lying on the grass. My boots crunch heavily on the hard gravel path, and I'm talking to myself as I walk, school bag bumping on my back. But the residents lodged on either side of these avenues won't complain about the noise.
>   They're dead.
>   Every one of them.
>
> *from **Whispers in the Graveyard** by Theresa Breslin*

2 **Third person**: the story is told from the point of view of someone outside the story. Characters are identified as: **she** or **he** (third person singular) or **they** (third person plural). For example:

> Sky, her little brother Chip, and her parents, had been sleeping in the car for months while they wandered back and forth across the country chasing rumours of work.
>   They had found some jobs, chopping wood or picking fruit, but nothing which lasted, or which paid enough to feed them all properly, let alone afford somewhere to sleep.
>   They'd never intended to become vagrants.
>
> *from **Throwaways** by Ian Strachan*

First and third person are the most common but there is another.

3 **Second person**: writing in the second person, 'you', is used far less often than first and third person – **you** (second person singular) or **you** (second person plural – more than one 'you'). Here is an example:

> You're walking down the street when you get that funny feeling – you know the one – that feeling that you're being watched. Even though you feel a little foolish you have to glance behind you, just to check it out. Usually there's no one there but you still can't shake off the feeling. It nags away at you.

Activity 3

Working in pairs, read the extracts below. For each one, decide whether the narrative perspective is first person, second person or third person.

Extract 1

When I called round at Sally's I showed her the paragraph in the *Westwich Evening News.*

'What do you think of that?' I asked her.

She read it, standing, and with an impatient frown on her pretty face.

'I don't believe it,' she said finally.

from 'Pawley's Peepholes' in **The Starlit Corridor** *by John Wyndham*

Extract 2

In Stoneygate there was a wilderness. It was an empty space between the houses and the river, where the ancient pit had been. That's where we played Askew's game, the game called Death. We used to gather at the school's gates after the bell had rung. We stood there whispering and giggling. After five minutes, Bobby Carr told us it was time and he led us through the wilderness to Askew's den.

from **Kit's Wilderness** *by David Almond*

Extract 3

It was almost December, and Jonas was beginning to be frightened. No. Wrong word, Jonas thought. Frightened meant that deep, sickening feeling of something terrible about to happen. Frightened was the way he had felt a year ago when an unidentified aircraft had overflown the community twice.

from **The Giver** *by Lois Lowry*

Extract 4

My father's family name being Pirrip, and my Christian name Philip, my infant tongue could make of both names nothing longer or more explicit than Pip. So, I called myself Pip, and came to be called Pip.

from **Great Expectations** *by Charles Dickens*

Choosing first person

The following short story is written in the first person. Work in pairs to do the activities that follow each part of the story.

W
p.199

Smart Ice-Cream

Well, I came top of the class again. One hundred out of one hundred for Maths. And one hundred out of one hundred for English. I'm just a natural brain, the best there is. There isn't one kid in the class who can come near me. Next to me they are all dumb.

5 Even when I was a baby I was smart. The day that I was born my mother started tickling me. 'Bub, bub, bub,' she said.

'Cut it out, Mum,' I told her. 'That tickles.' She nearly fell out of bed when I said that. I was very advanced for my age.

Every year I win a lot of prizes: top of the class, top of the school, stuff like that.
10 I won a prize for spelling when I was only three years old. I am a terrific speller. If you can say it, I can spell it. Nobody can trick me on spelling. I can spell every word there is.

Some kids don't like me; I know that for a fact. They say I'm a show-off. I don't care. They are just jealous because they are not as clever as me. I'm good-looking
15 too. That's another reason why they are jealous.

Activity 4

1 Look at how the writer has created a particular kind of first person narrator.

   ◆ How many times does the writer use the word 'I'?
   ◆ How many different boasts does the narrator make?

2 Think about your answers to those two questions and complete the following sentence: *To make the narrator seem big-headed and very boastful the writer does the following things: ...*

Now read on.

Last week something bad happened. Another kid got one hundred out of one hundred for Maths too. That never happened before – no one has ever done as well as me. I am always first on my own. A kid called Jerome Dadian beat me. He must have cheated. I was sure he cheated. It had something to do with that
20 ice-cream. I was sure of it. I decided to find out what was going on; I wasn't going to let anyone pull a fast one on me.

It all started with the ice-cream man, Mr Peppi. The old fool had a van which he parked outside the school. He sold ice-cream, all different types. He had every flavour there is, and some that I had never heard of before.

25 He didn't like me very much. He told me off once. 'Go to the back of the queue,' he said. 'You pushed in.'

'Mind your own business, Pop,' I told him. 'Just hand over the ice-cream.'

'No,' he said. 'I won't serve you unless you go to the back.'

30 I went round to the back of the van, but I didn't get in the queue. I took out a nail and made a long scratch on his rotten old van. He had just had it painted. Peppi came and had a look. Tears came into his eyes. 'You are a bad boy,' he said. 'One day you will get into trouble. You think you are smart. One day you will be too smart.'

35 I just laughed and walked off. I knew he wouldn't do anything. He was too soft-hearted. He was always giving free ice-creams to kids that had no money. He felt sorry for poor people. The silly fool.

Activity 5 🔷

We are given the **narrator's view** of Peppi and Jerome. Here is how you could describe the narrator's view of Jerome:

Give your opinion. —

> The narrator obviously does not like Jerome. He calls him 'kid' as though he is looking down on him. He tells us at least twice that Jerome must have 'cheated'.

— Support your opinion with evidence from the text.

1 Use the example above to explain how the narrator feels about Peppi.

2 Are your feelings about the characters different? What is *your* view of Peppi? Support your answer with some evidence from the story.

Now read on. As you read, pick out any new information and ideas we are given about the narrator's character. Make notes as you read.

There were a lot of stories going round about that ice-cream. People said that it was good for you. Some kids said that it made you better

40 when you were sick. One of the teachers called it 'Happy Ice-Cream'. I didn't believe it; it never made me happy.

All the same, there was something strange about it. Take Pimples Peterson for example. That wasn't his real name – I just called him that because he had a lot of pimples. Anyway, Peppi heard me calling

45 Peterson 'Pimples'. 'You are a real mean boy,' he said. 'You are always picking on someone else, just because they are not like you.'

'Get lost, Peppi,' I said. 'Go and flog your ice-cream somewhere else.'

Peppi didn't answer me. Instead he spoke to Pimples. 'Here, eat this,' he told him. He handed Peterson an ice-cream. It was the biggest ice-cream
50 I had ever seen. It was coloured purple. Peterson wasn't too sure about it. He didn't think he had enough money for such a big ice-cream.

'Go on,' said Mr Peppi. 'Eat it. I am giving it to you for nothing. It will get rid of your pimples.'

I laughed and laughed. Ice-cream doesn't get rid of pimples, it *gives*
55 you pimples. Anyway, the next day when Peterson came to school he had no pimples. Not one. I couldn't believe it. The ice-cream had cured his pimples.

There were some other strange things that happened too. There was a kid at the school who had a long nose. Boy, was it long. He looked like
60 Pinocchio. When he blew it you could hear it a mile away. I called him 'Snozzle'. He didn't like being called Snozzle. He used to go red in the face when I said it, and that was every time that I saw him. He didn't say anything back – he was scared that I would punch him up.

Peppi felt sorry for Snozzle too. He gave him a small green ice-cream
65 every morning, for nothing. What a jerk. He never gave me a free ice-cream.

You won't believe what happened but I swear it's true. Snozzle's nose began to grow smaller. Every day it grew a bit smaller. In the end it was just a normal nose. When it was the right size Peppi stopped giving him the green ice-creams.

Activity 6

1 What can you tell about the narrator from the following?

 ◆ What the narrator actually <u>says</u>, e.g. *'Get lost, Peppi,' I said* and *I called him 'Snozzle'. He didn't like being called Snozzle.*
 ◆ What the narrator <u>does</u>, e.g. *I laughed and laughed.*
 ◆ What <u>other characters feel</u>: *he was scared that I would punch him up.*
 ◆ What <u>other characters say</u>: *'You are a real mean boy.'*

2 Look at the notes you have made so far and use them to write down some thoughts on the following questions.

 ◆ What does the writer of this story want readers to think about his first person narrator?
 ◆ What have you learned about how a writer can create the 'character' of his/her narrator? What techniques can a writer use?

Now read the rest of the story.

70　I made up my mind to put a stop to this ice-cream business. Jerome Dadian had been eating ice-cream the day he got one hundred for Maths. It must have been the ice-cream making him smart. I wasn't going to have anyone doing as well as me. I was the smartest kid in the school, and that's the way I wanted it to stay. I wanted to get a look inside that ice-cream van to find out what was going on.

75　　I knew where Peppi kept his van at night – he left it in a small lane behind his house. I waited until about eleven o'clock at night. Then I crept out of the house and down to Peppi's van. I took a crowbar, a bucket of sand, a torch and some bolt cutters with me.

　　There was no one around when I reached the van. I sprang the door open with 80　the crowbar and shone my torch around inside. I had never seen so many tubs of ice-cream before. There was every flavour you could think of: there was apple and banana, cherry and mango, blackberry and watermelon and about fifty other flavours. Right at the end of the van were four bins with locks on them. I went over and had a look. It was just as I thought – these were his special flavours.

85　Each one had writing on the top. This is what they said:

　　　HAPPY ICE-CREAM for cheering people up.
　　　NOSE ICE-CREAM for long noses.
　　　PIMPLE ICE-CREAM for removing pimples.
　　　SMART ICE-CREAM for smart alecs.

90　　Now I knew his secret. That rat Dadian had been eating Smart Ice-Cream; that's how he got one hundred for Maths. I knew there couldn't be anyone as clever as me. I decided to fix Peppi up once and for all. I took out 95　the bolt cutters and cut the locks off the four bins; then I put sand into every bin in the van. Except for the Smart Ice-Cream. I didn't put any sand in that.

　　I laughed to myself. Peppi wouldn't sell much ice-cream now. Not unless he 100　started a new flavour – Sand Ice-Cream. I looked at the Smart Ice-Cream. I decided to eat some; it couldn't do any harm. Not that I needed it – I was already about as smart as you could get. Anyway, I gave it a try. I ate the lot. Once I started I couldn't stop. It tasted good. It was delicious.

　　I left the van and went home to bed, but I couldn't sleep. To tell the truth, 105　I didn't feel too good. So I decided to write this. Then if any funny business has been going on you people will know what happened. I think I have made a mistake. I don't think Dadian did get any Smart Ice-Cream.

　　It iz the nekst day now. Somefing iz hapening to me. I don't feal quite az smart. I have bean trying to do a reel hard sum. It iz wun and wun. Wot duz wun and 110　wun make? Iz it free or iz it for?

Smart Ice-Cream *by Paul Jennings*

Activity 7

1 What has happened to the narrator at the end of the story? In what ways has the narrator's language been changed?

2 How does the writer of the story want you to feel about what has happened to his narrator? Copy the chart below and decide which of the statements in the first column is most appropriate. Give reasons for your answer in the second column.

The statement	I agree or disagree because ...
He wants you to feel sorry for him.	
He wants you to feel angry that he has been tricked.	
He wants you to feel satisfied that he got what he deserved.	
He wants you to feel surprised because it was such a shock for you – there were no clues about what was going to happen.	

Activity 8

The punctuation used in this story is fairly straightforward. The narrator usually expresses himself in a fairly simple and direct way, as you can see for example from the start of the story. But, sometimes, a greater variety of punctuation than just full stops and commas is required. In this story, look at the writer's use of:

a semi-colons (;) in lines 13, 91 and 96
b colons (:) in lines 9 and 81.

Why do you think he chose to use colons and semi-colons at these points in the text? What effect does this punctuation have?

Based on these examples, write an explanation of when to use semi-colons and colons.

Using your own first person narrator

First person narrators don't have to be like the narrator in *Smart Ice-Cream*: they can have many different characteristics and can have different 'points of view' about the same events.

Activity 9 ICT WS

Look at the following story.

I'm really looking forward to starting my new school. It's going to be great

I hate this place and all those soppy little Year 7's.

1 You are going to write about what happened to the boy in the story from two different points of view:
   ◆ from the point of view of the young boy, and
   ◆ from the point of view of one of the two boys who pick on him.
   What happens is done for you in the cartoon strip. Concentrate on **how** to shows what your first person narrator is like. Think about:
   ◆ what he says ◆ what he does ◆ what other characters say and do.
   Each version of the story should only be a few sentences long. It should begin with the new boy's arrival at school and end with the two larger boys walking away.

2 Get your partner to read your two first drafts. Ask your partner to make notes on your drafts, using a table like the one below.

My impressions of ...	My evidence – the parts of the text that support my ideas
The young boy. He is: ◆ bright ◆ slightly nervous ◆ looking forward to starting at his new school.	
The older boy. He: ◆ hates school ◆ is big-headed ◆ has a reputation for being 'hard'.	

3 Ask your partner to comment on your spelling and punctuation.

4 When you have considered the response of your partner and made any necessary changes you should write a final draft of each version.

Using more than one narrator

Some stories may be told by more than one narrator. This can bring variety to writing because different narrators have different 'voices' and have a different perspective on events. It can allow you to structure a story in an interesting way.

Activity 10 ⓦ

You are going to write your own story with two different narrators.

Step 1: Read the descriptions of the plot and the narrators below.

The plot

It is the summer holidays and three or four young people are bored. They start to play tricks on a local elderly man. He lives on his own and has a quite large garden. The young people are able to climb over his wall. The man has a reputation among local children: he is considered to be a bit 'strange'.

The narrators

Your two narrators are to be (1) the old man and (2) one of the young people.

Step 2: Before you begin to write, you have to decide what kind of character each narrator is going to be. Copy the chart below and make notes on the questions.

What kind of character?	My notes
The elderly man Unfriendly and strange, lonely and shy? What kinds of words could he use? What kinds of things will he do?	
The young person Aggressive and uncaring or unhappy about what the young people are doing? What kinds of words could he or she use? What kinds of things will he or she do?	

Step 3: In Activities 4 to 9 you looked at how writers use language to create particular characters. It is very important in this piece of writing that you try to use different 'voices' for the two narrators. You should think about the following.

- **What** they talk about: the elderly man might focus on memories. Young people could refer to modern gadgets.
- **How** they talk: the young people might use slang and use shorter sentences.

Step 4: Now decide how to organise your plot. Remember to do the following.

- Keep the plot simple. There should only be two or three sections from each narrator. You could use a chart like the one below or make up your own.
- There could be further events. The story could end happily or in tragedy. Make sure you have some idea about your ending before you start to write.

Young person	Elderly man
1 The young people meet and chat. They decide to go to the old man's garden and steal some apples.	2 The old man is in his house doing something – he might be reading a letter or thinking about the past.
3 That evening our narrator tells us what happened in the garden. The old man saw them.	4 The old man tells us about what happened in the garden.

Step 5: You are ready to write the story.

- Your first draft should be a simple outline of what is going to happen, section by section.
- When you have completed your first draft, write the first two sections in full, concentrating on making the two voices sound different.
- Show this to a partner and ask him (or her) if he can see how you have made the two voices different. Change the writing if necessary.
- Then write the further sections. Show them to your partner for his (or her) opinion, and ask him to check your spelling and punctuation.
- When you have made all the corrections or improvements to your story, make a final copy.

This unit will help you to:

◆ write a range of non-fiction
◆ explore how non-fiction texts can convey information in an entertaining way
◆ consider the structure of paragraphs
◆ use language in imaginative ways.

Journalism

The following piece of writing is from the travel supplement of a Sunday newspaper. The writer has been investigating how useful different phrase books are when you are abroad on holiday. She tried out a Portuguese phrase book on a visit to Portugal and had some problems. As you read this part of the article for the first time, think about the following.

◆ What is the writer's attitude towards phrase books?
◆ Does she find them useful?

Lost for words —————— Headline.

Are phrase books a waste of time? Joanne O'Connor puts five of the best to the test while on holiday in Portugal — Sub-headline.

5   ['Pod rerkoomayndarmer ————— In phrase books
     algoonsh pratoosh   the foreign words
     rerzhyoonighsh?'] I ask hopefully.   are spelled in the
     The waiter smiles with the air of   way you
     one who has suffered much and   pronounce them.
10   turns on his heel. Moments later,
     he returns with a menu in
     English. 'The speciality is grilled
     sardines,' he says. I hide my
     Portuguese phrase book under
15   the table. 'OK, I'll have that.' And   In a way that
     then, inexplicably, I order a glass   can't be
     of white wine in Spanish, but   explained.
     with a French accent. That'll
     show him.

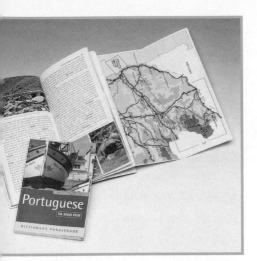

20   He returns with a huge carafe of wine. My   ⌐ A large bottle.
dilemma: whether to explain shamefacedly that   — Problem.
I only wanted a glass, which he would have
understood if I hadn't tried to show off by
speaking Spanish, or pretend I meant to
25 order it and drink the whole carafe. I decide
the latter is easier.   — The last-mentioned
    Having just spent a weekend in Lisbon   one – i.e. she'll
putting a handful of Portuguese phrase books   pretend she
through their paces, I can confirm that, where   ordered it.
30 foreign languages are concerned, a little bit of
knowledge is a dangerous thing. Apart from
anything else, there is something
fundamentally naff about using a phrase book. — Very 'uncool'.
Like guide books, cameras and sunburn, they
35 confer on the user an instant badge of shame: — Give or bestow.
'Look at me everyone, I'm a tourist.' Surely it's
better to be lost and misunderstood than
causing patisserie queue rage as you insist on — Cake shop.
looking up the word for custard tart.
40   You can try to get around this by secretly
swotting up on a few key phrases and keeping
the book out of sight, but even this can backfire
horribly. Before joining the ticket queue in the
metro, I rehearsed: 'A return ticket to Oriente,
45 please', only to be told in Portuguese that this — Underground
particular metro line was still under   railway.
construction (though obviously I didn't
understand this was what he was saying at
the time).
50   By the time you have looked this one up in
your phrase book, a) you will have been lynched — Attacked.
by an angry mob, b) the man behind the counter
will have pulled down the blind and gone home,
or c) if you are really lucky the line will have
55 been completed. The moral of this story: speak
perfect Portuguese to people and they will
answer you in perfect Portuguese, which is not
much good if you can't speak the language.

*from the 'Escape' section of the **Observer**,*
12 August 2001

Activity 1 ICT WS

1 Work in pairs. Copy and complete the chart below to explore your first ideas about the writer's attitude towards the use of phrase books. Decide whether you agree or disagree with each statement about the writer's attitude and use the third column to note down your evidence. An example has been done for you.

The writer's attitude	Agree/Disagree	Evidence
She: ◆ thinks phrase books are easy to use	Disagree	The long complicated words at the beginning show how difficult they are to use.
◆ finds them useful		
◆ thinks they lead to embarrassing situations		
◆ takes the whole subject very seriously		

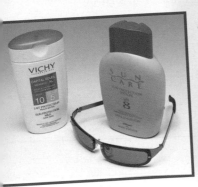

2 When you have completed the chart, discuss with your partner which of the following statements you agree with most.

a The writer's main purpose is to give readers information about phrase books.

b The writer wants to entertain her readers and that is her main aim.

Decide between you **why** you find one statement more acceptable than the other and write down your reason so that it can be shared with the rest of the class.

Making writing easy to follow

The extract from 'Lost for Words' (pages 56–57) shows how structure is as important in non-fiction as in fiction to make it interesting and easy to follow. The writer of the newspaper article has used various features particular to this form of writing (such as headline, sub-headline), as well as techniques common to other forms (paragraphs, logical sequence of sentences).

Activity 2 (ws)

Work on the following with a partner. Make notes of your answers as you work.

1 The extract from 'Lost for Words' begins with a headline and a sub-headline. What is the purpose of the sub-headline? What important information does it give the reader?

2 The writing is broken down into paragraphs to help readers. Each paragraph should be about a new stage or idea in the writing. Copy and fill in the following flow chart to show how the writer's ideas move forward. Sum up each paragraph.

3 Inside a paragraph, sentences should follow each other logically. Here are the four sentences from the third paragraph. Copy and complete the table below with your own notes.

The four sentences	The 'idea'
Having just spent a weekend in Lisbon putting a handful of Portuguese phrase books through their paces, I can confirm that, where foreign languages are concerned, a little bit of knowledge is a dangerous thing.	This first sentence introduces the main idea or topic of the paragraph: that relying on a phrase book can bring problems.
Apart from anything else, there is something fundamentally naff about using a phrase book.	This sentence gives the first problem: that …
Like guide books, cameras and sunburn, they confer on the user an instant badge of shame: 'Look at me everyone, I'm a tourist.'	This sentence explains the problem in more detail. The problem is …
Surely it's better to be lost and misunderstood than causing patisserie queue rage as you insist on looking up the word for custard tart.	This sentence gives an example of the kind of problem caused by use of phrase books …

4 Use the writer's framework to write your own paragraph of four sentences in which you follow an idea. You could use the openings of the writer's sentences, for example:

> Having just *bought a CD, I would like to complain about the service I received in the shop.* Apart from anything else, *I think I was charged too much.* Like *lots of other goods, CDs seem to be more expensive here than in other countries.* Surely *it's about time we did something about this.*

Work with a partner to construct your own four-sentence paragraph using the same sentence introductions.

> ◆ Having just … ◆ Apart from anything else … ◆ Like … ◆ Surely …

Engaging the reader

The writer of 'Lost for Words' does a number of things with language to 'hook' her readers and make the writing interesting for them.

Activity 3 WS

Discuss with a partner the things the writer does (listed in the chart) and make a note of your responses.

What the writer does	She does this because ...
She begins with some very odd, difficult words.	She wants to grab the reader's attention.
She uses little stories. There are at least two.	
She uses the first person 'I' to tell us about her experiences, but she changes to the second person, 'You' in the later paragraphs.	
She uses some surprising phrases like 'patisserie queue rage'.	

Travel writing

The writer of 'Lost for Words' (pages 56–57) is a journalist. In her article, she focuses on phrase books and whether they are useful. In Activities 1 to 3 you looked at her attitude and her techniques for making her writing entertaining. Now you are going to examine these aspects of writing in another non-fiction form.

In the following extract the writer describes an experience he has in Rome. Think about which of the following statements best describes his attitude towards the way Italians park.

- ◆ He thinks the way they park is something for us all to admire and copy.
- ◆ He actually hates the way they park – he is being sarcastic.
- ◆ He means that he finds their way of parking is very entertaining.

Devastating parking

I love the way the Italians park. You turn any street corner in Rome and it looks as if you've just missed a parking competition for blind people. Cars are pointed in every direction, half on the pavements and half off, facing in, facing sideways, blocking garages and side streets and phone boxes, fitted into spaces so tight that
5 the only possible way out would be through the sun roof. Romans park their cars the way I would park if I had just spilled a beaker of **hydrochloric acid** on my lap.

  I was strolling along the **Via Sistina** one morning when a **Fiat Croma** shot past and screeched to a smoky halt a hundred feet up the road. Without pause the driver lurched into reverse and came barrelling backwards down the street in the
10 direction of a parking space that was precisely the length of his Fiat, less two and a half feet. Without slowing even fractionally, he veered the car into the space and crashed resoundingly into a parked **Renault**.

  Nothing happened for a minute. There was just the hiss of escaping steam. Then the driver leaped from his car, gazed in **profound** disbelief at the devastation before
15 him – crumpled metal, splintered tail lights, the exhaust pipe of his own car limply grazing the pavement – and regarded it with as much mystification as if it had dropped on him from the sky. Then he did what I suppose almost any Italian would do. He kicked the Renault in the side as hard as he could,
20 denting the door, punishing its absent owner for having the **gall** to park there, then leaped back in his Fiat and drove off as madly as he had arrived, and peace returned once again to the Via Sistina, apart from the occasional clank of a piece of metal dropping off the stricken Renault. No one
25 but me batted an eye.

*from **Neither Here Nor There** by Bill Bryson*

Word bank
hydrochloric acid – a very strong acid
Via Sistina – famous street in Rome
Fiat Croma – popular Italian car
Renault – popular French car
profound – great or deep
gall – courage or cheek

Activity 4

Explain what the three stages of this piece of writing are by completing the following:

> The first paragraph is like an introduction to the general topic of Italian
> car-parking. The second paragraph moves on to ....
> The third paragraph ....

Developing a comic approach

Bill Bryson wants readers to find the writing amusing and uses language for comic effects.

Activity 5 ⒾⒸⓉ ⓌⓈ

Work with a partner. Discuss the following uses of language. Note your ideas.

1   The writer makes funny comparisons using 'as if'. The ideas that follow 'as if' are quite far-fetched. Copy and complete the chart below.

The writer's words	The effect
'it looks as if <u>you've just missed a parking competition for blind people</u>.'	This is funny because you realise that if people couldn't see then their parking would be a disaster: you can visualise how chaotic it would be. It's a very amusing picture.
'Romans park their cars the way I would park if <u>I had just spilled a beaker of hydrochloric acid on my lap</u>.'	
'regarded it with as much mystification as if <u>it had dropped on him from the sky</u>.'	

2   The writer uses carefully chosen verbs to make the scene he is describing more dramatic. These are underlined for you in the paragraph below.

   ◆   The verbs are all about movement. One verb contrasts strongly with the others. Which one is it? How does the contrast help make the writing more amusing?

   ◆   Think about what the writer is trying to say about this Italian's driving.

   Why does he use so many verbs that are quite exaggerated?

I <u>was strolling</u> along the Via Sistina one morning when a Fiat Croma <u>shot</u> past and <u>screeched</u> to a smoky halt a hundred feet up the road. Without pause the driver <u>lurched</u> into reverse and came <u>barrelling</u> backwards down the street in the direction of a parking space that was precisely the length of his Fiat, less two and a half feet. Without slowing even fractionally, he <u>veered</u> the car into the space and <u>crashed</u> resoundingly into a parked Renault.

You have looked at how two writers:

◆ have an 'attitude' towards the subject, a particular point of view
◆ organise their writing into paragraphs to help readers follow the ideas
◆ use language in a variety of ways to interest, entertain or amuse the reader.

You are now going to attempt your own short piece of writing.

Activity 6 WS

Write three paragraphs in which you describe a place in an amusing way.

Step 1: First choose a place. Here are some ideas that might help.

◆ Your own house. Perhaps you could describe your house at breakfast time when people are rushing around trying to get ready.
◆ Your school canteen. You might want to poke fun at the chaos or at the noise.
◆ A holiday beach with all the strange shapes, sizes and behaviours seen there.

You could use a table like the one below to help you shape your ideas.

Location	Time of day	Activity	People involved	Humour	Compare to
E.g. own house	Breakfast time	Rushing around	Family	Accidents caused by rushing	Like a circus act

Step 2: Next you might make a framework like this.

Paragraph	Content
1	Make an opening statement that introduces my general point. For example: Beaches are a bit like zoos …
2	Outline a little story that gives detail to my general point. For example: The beach in St Ives was buzzing on a hot August day …
3	Develop the comparison with zoos: There were people jumping around like chimps …

Step 3: Write a first draft of the three paragraphs. Check that you have used some of the features listed below that you explored in Activities 3 and 5.

◆ using a startling opening to hook the reader   ◆ using little stories
◆ using interesting comparisons   ◆ exaggerating by using well-chosen verbs.

Step 4: If you have not used at least two of the features above change your draft.

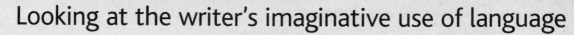

Looking at the writer's imaginative use of language

Writers of non-fiction use language in the same kinds of imaginative ways as the writers of fiction and poetry. The following piece of writing is another example of the genre of travel writing but it is very different from Bill Bryson's comic writing on page 61.

As you read the text, focus on the writer's choice of detail and how she uses language in an interesting way to make the experience come to life for the reader.

Exotic dawn

W
p.199

The wide flat river went snaking through dense tangled mighty forest; trees tall and majestic, roped together with knotted vines, strung with white flowering creeper; branches hung shaggy with green trailing **lichen**, and **enshrouded** in
5 cobweb; straight trees with pale luminous pinky-yellow bark, short **squat** trees with leaves like fans, or feathers; trees with leaves the size of umbrellas; **gnarled** old and crooked trees; immense trees 100 feet tall with roots like the fins of rocket ships; **impenetrable** dark undergrowth; monkeys fighting
10 and thunder rumbling; parrots and **hornbills** flying overhead; hot and sultry sun; the smell of sweating earth in the forest, and the perfume of flowers hanging heavily in the air.

Christina Dodwell, from **The Virago Book of Women Travellers**

Word bank

lichen – a type of plant
enshrouded – covered
squat – small and thick
gnarled – knobbly, twisted
impenetrable – that can't be seen or walked through
hornbills – birds of the tropics

Activity 7 ICT WS

You are going to examine how the writer has created an effective description.

1 **The use of adjectives.** The writer uses a lot of adjectives to describe the forest and trees. A list of the adjectives might begin with *dense, tangled*. Complete the list.

2 Which of the following reasons might best explain her use of adjectives?
   a The forest was very simple so she wanted to make it sound more interesting.
   b She is a writer and good writers use lots of descriptive words.
   c She is trying to give the reader as detailed and vivid a picture of the forest as possible.

3 **The use of comparisons.** The writer compares various parts of the forest to snakes, fans, feathers, shrouds, umbrellas and the fins of rocket ships. Choose two of those images and write about their effectiveness. Here is an example:

> 'The wide flat river went snaking through dense tangled mighty forest. This image, comparing the river to a snake, is a good one. It gives a picture of the river bending through the jungle just like a snake bends its body around objects. You find snakes in the jungle so it seems very appropriate. There is also a slight sense of danger: snakes can be a little frightening.

This unit will help you to:
- write in different forms of poetry
- explore how form shapes meaning.

Writing poetry: being aware of different forms

Whenever you have an idea you wish to explore in writing, you are faced with a great range of choices. How will you express your idea? In what form? You could jot something in a diary, write a letter, type an e-mail, write a poem or a story. Often we write in a particular form because we have been told to, but ideas may be developed in a variety of ways.

Starting small

Texts come in all shapes and sizes – some of them very short! It is possible to write poems that are nothing but titles. Here is an example:

MEMORIES OF LAST NIGHT'S REVISION: A POEM

That is intended to be comic: the point is that *nothing* can be remembered.

Here is another example:

A POEM ABOUT ALL THE THINGS I LOVE ABOUT VEGETABLES

Again the point is that the writer of the poem likes *nothing* about vegetables.

Both of these examples are intended as mild jokes, but it may be possible to make a serious point about an issue, for example:

THE WHALE'S FUTURE: A POEM

If nothing follows that, it suggests there is no future for the whale.

Activity 1

Write three of your own poems that consist of only a title. Write a mixture of the funny and the serious.

1 To get started, think of something that you don't like, such as a football team you don't like. Your poem could be called 'What I Like About …' with nothing following.

2 Then think of things that might not have much of a future, such as an endangered species, or your good intentions to do your homework.

Keeping it short

You don't always have to write at great length to express an idea. It's often more effective to write very concisely. Here is a poem in which the writer explores a quite common phrase ('capital punishment' means the death penalty).

Poem Against Capital Punishment

I live in the capital
and it's punishment

Roger McGough

The poem is based on looking at a fairly common phrase in a new way. Interesting ideas can be generated by trying something as simple and short as that.

You can write your own very short poems based on simple little phrases. For example, the phrase 'hi-fi' is a short-hand phrase for a sound system, but it can be turned into a poem. 'Hi' sounds like a greeting and 'fi' is part of the pantomime poem, 'Fee, fi fo, fum / I smell the blood of an Englishman.' So a little poem can be developed.

HI-FI

Hi!
Have you seen Fee?
Or Fo?
Or, whatsisname, um?

Activity 2

Write three brief poems based on a new look at some of the following phrases, or use your own.

The phrase	Some ideas
COMPUTER MOUSE	Write about a real mouse rather than a piece of computer equipment, e.g.: *Computer crashed.* *The man at the repair shop said* *Something had nibbled through the Cables.* *A computer mouse?*
FAST FOOD	Think of entertaining ideas for zooming vegetables or animals speeding away from the butcher.
MOBILE PHONE	Write about a phone able to move by itself.
SECOND-CLASS POST	Change the meaning of 'post' to the kind of post that is stuck in the ground – like a pole.
CRIME FIGURES	Write about the various shapes of members of a gang.

Adding shape: lines and syllables

The short poems you wrote in Activity 2 did not have to be in any particular shape.

One way of shaping a poem is to use a precise number of lines and a particular number of syllables in a line. Syllables are the parts of a word that can be pronounced separately, for example 'word' (one syllable); 'pan–to–mime' (three syllables).

Cinquains are poems which, as you can guess if you know your French numbers, have five lines. The five lines have to contain a pattern of syllables: 2, 4, 6, 8, 2. Here is an example.

Cinquain

And so
As evening falls
I close the curtains on
The empty bed. And shadows creep
5 Inside.

Valerie Bloom

Activity 3 ICT WS

Now you are going to write your own cinquains.

> **Plan your poem.**

Begin with an idea for a pair of short lines to start and finish your poem to give yourself a framework for planning how to develop your cinquain. For example, suppose you decide on an opening line of two syllables, 'Tra–ffic.'

Think: where do you find traffic? In the 'City'. What is the connection between traffic and the city? A traffic jam.

That thought could be developed: traffic is a problem in busy cities.
So you could write a poem like this:

Traffic
Slowly grinding
To a halt. Clogging and
Blocking the arteries of the
City.

> **Follow the steps below to write your cinquains.**

Step 1: Choose one of the following pairs of opening/last lines.

- ◆ Sunshine/Morning
- ◆ Dark clouds/Sadness
- ◆ My mum/My friend
- ◆ Birthday/Happy

Step 2: Now think about what you will put in the three lines between the first and last. Use a frame like the one below and write your ideas in the middle.

SUNSHINE ⟶ ⟶ MORNING

Step 3: Write the three middle lines of the poem, remembering to use the correct number of syllables. These are very short poems so try to avoid repeating words or overusing words like 'the' or 'and' which don't carry much meaning. There are always several ways of making lines fit the pattern of syllables. Look at the 'Traffic' example again. Notice that you can't stop at the end of the third line, at 'and'. You have to read on without a pause.

> *Traffic*
> *Slowly grinding*
> *To a halt. Clogging and*
> *Blocking the arteries of the*
> *City.*

Step 4: Check your work and make a final copy of the whole poem.

Activity 4

Now that you have written one cinquain, you can use the same pattern of poem to develop more surprising ideas and see where the pattern of the poem takes your thinking.

Step 1: Work with a partner. Each of you should write a numbered list of ten two-syllable words/phrases. Make your list a mixture of:

◆ nouns (e.g. winter, pavements, paper)
◆ adverbs (e.g. softly, briefly, calmly)
◆ adjectives + noun (e.g. red shoes, thin legs, fast cars).

Keep your list to yourself; don't tell your partner the words on the list.

Step 2: When you have both completed your lists, each of you says two numbers between one and ten. Your partner will tell you which words on his or her list you have selected. Your task is to write a cinquain in which those words are the first and last lines.

You will need to use some imagination to make a connection. If you were given the following: 'paper' and 'thin legs', you might end up with something like:

> *Thin legs*
> *Furiously*
> *Sprint to the finish line.*
> *Pain worth it for his name in the*
> *Paper.*

Step 3: If you get really stuck with the combination you are given, then ask for a replacement number and change one of the pair.

Step 4: When you have written your cinquain share it with your partner. Let him or her check that you have got the pattern of syllables correct.

Adding shape through rhyme

Cinquains don't rhyme, unlike a lot of poems and songs. Rhyme brings pattern to poetry. It can make lines easier to remember by the repetition of similar or identical sounds.

Just as having a pattern of syllables in your cinquain made you shape your ideas in a particular way, rhyme also makes you take decisions about how to express thoughts. You may know the following traditional rhyme.

Little Boys

What are little boys made of?
Frogs and snails
And puppy-dogs' tails
That's what little boys are made of.

It uses repetition and rhyme, and trips off the tongue largely because of the two rhyming lines in the middle.

Activity 5 ICT

1 Adapt the shape of 'Little Boys' to write your own simple poem to see how using rhyme shapes what you say. Either:

a keep the subject, 'Little Boys' and write a modern version or a non-sexist version in which you will change the two middle lines, or

b choose your own subject: it might be 'Little Girls' or 'Fathers' or 'Teachers'. For example, you might write:

> **English Teachers**
> *What are English teachers made of?*
> *Poems and plays*
> *And wall displays*
> *That's what English teachers are made of.*

2 When you have written a first draft of your poem, show it to a partner. Discuss whether your poem makes an interesting point. Is it funny? Is it true?

Rhyme can add impact, to help poets make quite serious points. Read 'The Common and the Goose' which protests that the rich are treated better than the poor.

The Common and the Goose

The law locks up the man or woman
Who steals the goose from off the **common**
But leaves the greater **felon** loose
Who steals the common from the goose.

Anonymous

Word bank

common – common land traditionally used for grazing animals
felon – criminal

This protest poem is putting forward the idea that people who commit little crimes – like stealing a goose – are treated harshly, but bigger criminals, who 'steal the common from the goose' (buy up land and take it from poor people) go unpunished. The poem uses rhyme at the end of each pair of lines. These are called 'rhyming couplets'. Rhyme like this is very suited to short poems: it has a punchy effect and seems to sum up an idea.

Adding shape through rhythm

It is not just rhyme that brings a pattern. Count the syllables in each line of the 'The Common and the Goose'. What do you notice?

You may also notice that poems often have strong rhythms which come from the pattern of syllables. The poem may be read in a 'ti tum ti tum ti tum ti tum' rhythm:

The **law** locks **up** the **man** or **wom**an
Who **steals** the **goose** from **off** the **comm**on
But **leaves** the **great**er **fel**on **loose**
Who **steals** the **comm**on **from** the **goose**.

There are four beats – stressed syllables – in each line.

In the English language, where words have more than one syllable we stress one syllable more than others. For example, we say '**Eng**lish', '**green**house', 'com**put**er'. In Britain we say 'de**fence**' whereas in America they stress a different syllable: they say '**de**fence'.

Activity 6 ICT

1   Write out the following words using capitals or a different colour to show which syllable is stressed.

◆ weather	◆ reference	◆ daffodil	◆ mobile	◆ London

2   Do the same with the following lines of poetry. Work out the rhythm and write out the lines using colour or capital letters to show the stressed syllables.

'Andy Pandy, fine and dandy'	'The world is round, so travellers tell,'
'Double, double toil and trouble'	'Dance to your daddy, / My little babby'

3   Now write a single line of poetry that has four beats (stressed syllables) and may be read in a pattern – ti tum ti tum ti tum ti tum. It must have eight syllables. For example:

The **foot**ball **match** was **fierce** and **tense**

Choose any subject you wish. When you have written your line, share it with a partner so that he or she can check that it fits the pattern.

4   Then, still working in pairs, choose either your line or your partner's line and try to write a second line that will rhyme with it (best to pick the line that seems easiest to find a rhyme for!). For example, the line above could be continued:

The **foot**ball **match** was **fierce** and **tense**   With **fast** at**tack** and **strong** de**fence**.

Activity 7 (ws)

Working with a partner, write a short protest poem in rhyming couplets. Make it **four** lines long so that you use **two** rhyming couplets. Try to have the same number of syllables in each line.

Here are some ideas. You could protest about:

◆ the amount of homework you get
◆ school uniform
◆ the gap between rich and poor people
◆ the way some animals are treated
◆ the ways young people are treated.

Step 1: Think of an idea for something you wish to protest about. Use one of the ideas above or choose your own topic for protest.

Step 2: Jot down a few ideas about *why* you feel something is wrong.

Step 3: Write a first line. As you write it, think very carefully about rhyme. For example, if you decided to write a protest about homework you might quickly write something like: *I think I have too much homework*. That leaves you with the problem of finding an effective rhyme for 'homework'. You might think of 'shirk', but you could struggle to find rhymes. There are solutions.

◆ Change your line so that it ends with a different word. If you changed your line to: 'I get too much homework from my school', it would be easier to rhyme with.

◆ If you decide it is important to end the line with the key word 'homework', you could use rhyme that isn't perfect. For example, words that end in a 'k' sound, like 'luck' or an 'rk' sound, like 'dark' might give you some ideas.

Step 4: When you have roughly worked out your two rhyming couplets, read them aloud and think about the rhythm. Try to work a pattern of beats into your lines and make it the same pattern in each line.

Step 5: Show your poem to another pair and ask them to comment on the following.

◆ Is the 'point' of the poem clear? Is it easy to see what the protest is?
◆ Is it easy to read in a particular rhythm?
◆ Are the rhyming words important words or do they just seem to be there because they rhyme?

Using patterns in longer poems

Poets use rhyme and rhythm in longer poems as well. Read the following poem by John Agard. It is written in couplets and uses a refrain (a repeated section). As you read it look for any other words and phrases that are repeated and form a pattern. For example, the phrase 'Who is de girl' is repeated often.

Who is de Girl?

Who is de girl dat kick de ball
then jump for it over de wall

sallyann is a girl so full-o zest
sallyann is a girl dat just can't rest

5 who is de girl dat pull de hair
of de bully and make him scare

sallyann is a girl so full-o zest
sallyann is a girl dat just can't rest

who is de girl dat bruise she knee
10 when she fall from de mango tree

sallyann is a girl so full-o zest
sallyann is a girl dat just can't rest

who is de girl dat set de pace
when boys and girls dem start to race

15 sallyann is a girl so full-o zest
sallyann is a girl dat just can't rest.

John Agard

Did you notice the following patterns?

◆ The non-refrain stanzas always begin in exactly the same way.
◆ Each line in the non-refrain stanzas contains eight syllables.

Activity 8

Work in groups of three or four to prepare a reading aloud of 'Who is de Girl?'.

1 One person or one pair of you should read the refrain while someone else reads the other lines. Decide who will read which sections.

2 It is important to try to capture a rhythm when reading the poem aloud. Discuss each line as a group to decide how the line should be read. For example, would it make better sense to read the first line in the first or second way:

> ◆ Who **is** de **girl** dat **kick** de **ball** ◆ **Who** is de **girl** dat **kick** de **ball**

Which word is more important: 'Who' or 'is'?

3 When you have talked and practised, read your version aloud to the class.

Activity 9

Use 'Who is de Girl?' as a model to write your own patterned poem.

Step 1: The subject of your poem should be a real or made-up person whose name should be used in the refrain. John Agard's poem is about a girl full of life and energy; you need a similar focus or characteristic. You might write about a person who is accident-prone, or very intelligent or forgetful. For example:

> *Ellie's a girl so cheerful and loud*
> *Ellie's a girl stands out in the crowd*

Step 2: When you have chosen a person and worked out the characteristic you are going to explore, the next stage is to write four couplets that give examples of that characteristic – just as John Agard gave examples of sallyann's 'zest' for life. So, for example, you might write:

> *Who is the girl always on the phone*
> *Lots of mates, never on her own.*
>
> *Ellie's a girl so cheerful and loud*
> *Ellie's a girl stands out in the crowd*

Step 3: When you have written a draft of your four stanzas and the repeated refrain you should look through it to consider improvements. The example about 'Ellie' shown above could be improved: the first line, *Who is the girl always on the phone*, contains nine syllables whereas the second line has eight. To make the lines the same length it would be easy to rewrite the first line as: *Who's the girl always on the phone*. Alternatively, the second line could have an added syllable: *Has lots of mates, never on her own.*

Step 4: When you feel your poem is finished, read it aloud to a partner.

In units 5, 6 and 7 you have been developing your ability to write to imagine, explore and entertain. This assignment will test your ability to use some of the skills you have developed.

Autobiographical writing

Writing about yourself is not a simple matter of writing down some facts. Autobiographical writing needs to be shaped and written with other readers in mind. Laurie Lee's *Cider with Rosie* is a famous autobiography about childhood in the early part of the twentieth century. In the following extract the writer remembers his village school.

Village school

Our village school was poor and crowded, but in the end I **relished** it. It had a lively reek of steaming life: boys' boots, girls' hair, stoves and sweat, blue ink, white chalk and shavings. We learnt nothing **abstract** or **tenuous** there – just simple patterns of facts and letters, portable tricks of calculation, no more than was needed to
5 measure a shed, write out a bill, read a swine-disease warning. Through the dead hours of the morning, through the long afternoons, we chanted away at our tables. Passers-by could hear our rising voices in our bottled-up room on the bank: 'Twelve-inches-one-foot. Three-feet-make-a-yard. Fourteen-pounds-make-a-stone. Eight-stone-a-hundred-weight.' We absorbed these figures as **primal** truths declared
10 by some ultimate power. Unhearing, unquestioning, we rocked to our chanting, hammering the gold nails home. 'Twice-two-are-four. One-God-is-Love. One-Lord-is-King. One-King-is-Fifth …' So it was always; had been, would be for ever; we asked no questions; we didn't hear what we said; yet neither did we ever forget it.

from Cider with Rosie by Laurie Lee

Word bank
relished – really enjoyed
abstract – ideas, not physical matter
tenuous – of little substance
primal – basic or primitive

Laurie Lee gives readers **lots of details** to help them share the sights and sounds of his village school.

Write a piece called 'Memories' in which you share with the reader some memories from your childhood. You should concentrate on the following.

◆ Use details to help the reader see and hear the events you are describing.
◆ Use interesting words and different kinds of sentences to bring variety to the writing.
◆ Organise what you write into clearly organised and developed paragraphs. Make a paragraph plan before you start to write. You could use a chart like the one below.

Paragraph	Content
1	My earliest memories before school
2	Being in the Infants
3	Moving up to Junior school

Section C ◆ Reading non-fiction and media texts
Introduction

Non-fiction texts are not poems, stories, novels or plays. They are not made up. They include letters, journals, articles and advertisements. 'The media' is the name given to types of communication that reach large numbers of people. Some examples of different types of media are television, radio, the Internet and newspapers.

In Year 8 you will have examined a range of non-fiction and media texts, distinguishing between fact, opinion and theory, identifying argument and developing awareness of the author's point of view. You will have considered the importance of presentation and developed your own research skills.

You will be building on these skills in the units in this section.

In Unit 9, *Thinking about points of view*, you will examine a range of autobiographical writing. You will think about how writers' styles vary. You will identify the points of view offered on people and society, and compare the ways emotions are shown in two autobiographies.

In Unit 10, *Investigating advertising*, you will identify how meaning is conveyed through print and images. You will think about the link between content, purpose and audience. You will also consider the ways advertising affects our lives.

In Unit 11, *Recognising bias*, you will learn how to distinguish between objectivity and bias. You will examine how a writer can use language to show bias. You will also evaluate the reliability of a newspaper article.

Unit 12 tests you on the skills you will develop as you work carefully through the three units.

This unit will help you to:

◆ review and develop your own reading

◆ become more aware of different styles of writing

◆ use notes for representing information

◆ recognise social and historical detail

◆ consider how ideas and feelings are explored.

Looking at autobiography

One form of non-fiction is autobiography. An autobiography is an account of a person's life written by that person. As a class, list any autobiographies you have read or know of. What different kinds of people write autobiographies? Can you recommend to other class members any of the autobiographies you have read? If so, which ones and why? Keep a copy of your list.

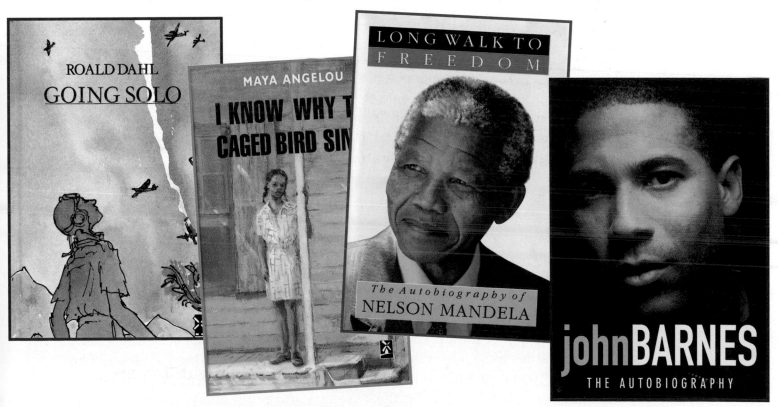

Finding out about the writer

Autobiographies are usually written in chronological (date) order, starting with the writer's childhood. The opening often tells you something about the kind of person the writer is and the culture in which he or she grew up.

Activity 1

Read the autobiography opening below and on the next page. Make notes in a chart like the one below on what you learn.

Details in the opening	*Chinese Cinderella*
Gender of writer, i.e. male/female	
Age of writer at the start	
Background information, e.g. country, language, family	
The event described	
Important relationships	
Important life events	

Chinese Cinderella

Autumn, 1941.

As soon as I got home from school, Aunt Baba noticed the silver medal
dangling from the left breast-pocket of my uniform.

'What's that hanging on your dress?'

'It's something special that Mother Agnes gave me in front of the whole
5 class this afternoon. She called it an award.'

My aunt looked thrilled. 'So soon? You only started kindergarten one week
ago. What is it for?'

'It's for topping my class this week. When Mother Agnes pinned it on my
dress, she said I could wear it for seven days. Here, this certificate goes with it.'
10 I opened my school-bag and handed her an envelope as I climbed onto
her lap.

She opened the envelope and took out the certificate.

'Why, it's all written in French or English or some other foreign language.
How do you expect me to read this, my precious little treasure?' I knew she
15 was pleased because she was smiling as she hugged me. 'One day soon,' she
continued, 'you'll be able to translate all this into Chinese for me. Until then,
we'll just write today's date on the envelope and put it away somewhere safe.'

I watched her open her **closet** door and take out her safe-deposit box. She
took the key from a gold chain around her neck and placed my certificate
20 underneath her jade bracelet, pearl necklace and diamond watch – as if my
award were also some precious jewel impossible to replace.

p.205

As she closed the lid, an old photograph fell out. I picked up the faded picture and saw a solemn young man and woman, both dressed in old-fashioned Chinese robes. The man looked rather familiar.

25 'Is this a picture of my father and dead mama?' I asked.

'No. This is the wedding picture of your grandparents. Your **Ye Ye** was twenty-six and your **Nai Nai** was only fifteen.' She quickly took the photo from me and locked it in her box.

'Do you have a picture of my dead mama?'

30 She avoided my eyes. 'No. But I have wedding pictures of your father and stepmother Niang. You were only one year old when they married. Do you want to see them?'

'No. I've seen those before. I just want to see one of my own mama. Do I look like her?' Aunt Baba did not reply, but busied herself putting the safe-deposit
35 box back into her closet. After a while I said, 'When did my mama die?'

'Your mother came down with a high fever three days after you were born. She died when you were two weeks old …' She hesitated for a moment, then exclaimed suddenly, 'How dirty your hands are! Have you been playing in that sand-box at school again? Go wash them at once! Then come back and do
40 your homework!'

I did as I was told. Though I was only four years old, I understood I should not ask Aunt Baba too many questions about my dead mama. Big Sister once told me, 'Aunt Baba and Mama used to be best friends. A long time ago, they worked together in a bank in Shanghai owned by our Grand Aunt, the
45 youngest sister of Grandfather Ye Ye. But then Mama died giving birth to you. If you had not been born, Mama would still be alive. She died because of you. You are bad luck.'

*adapted from **Chinese Cinderella** by Adeline Yen Mah*

Word bank
closet – a cupboard or storeroom
Ye Ye – paternal grandfather
Nai Nai – paternal grandfather's wife

Activity 2 ICT WS

1 Use the notes you made in Activity 1 to help you write two paragraphs about the writer of *Chinese Cinderella*. You could organise your ideas by linking details like this:

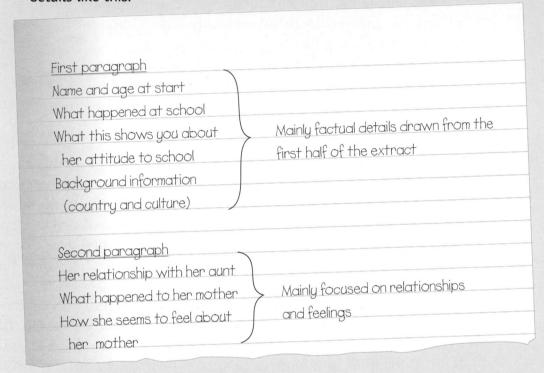

First paragraph
Name and age at start
What happened at school
What this shows you about
 her attitude to school
Background information
 (country and culture)

Mainly factual details drawn from the first half of the extract

Second paragraph
Her relationship with her aunt
What happened to her mother
How she seems to feel about
 her mother

Mainly focused on relationships and feelings

2 Here is an example of how you could organise your ideas in your first paragraph. Different colours show how the sentences are linked in different ways. If you copy it, you will need to fill in the spaces.

The writer of Chinese Cinderella is .... The first incident she

recalls in her autobiography was when she was .... years old.

This was when she received............... for .... Her aunt was

very .... with her. This shows that both she and her aunt thought

education was .... We also find out that she is ....

Her aunt only speaks ...., and her grandparents are called her

.... and ....

3 Now write the second paragraph. Make clear links between your sentences. When you have finished, re-read your paragraph. Highlight the links you have made.

Writing autobiography in the first person

In *Chinese Cinderella* the writer uses the first person.
This means she uses 'I' when writing about her life.
Autobiographies are often written in the first person.

> As soon as I got home from school, Aunt Baba
> noticed the silver medal dangling from the left
> breast-pocket of my uniform.

Activity 3 ICT WS

Talk with a partner about the advantages and disadvantages of writing in the
first person. Below are some statements. Decide:

- ◆ if you agree with them
- ◆ if they are advantages or disadvantages.

> It lets you get inside the mind of the writer.

> It makes it seem real because the writer is describing her own life.

> The writer is able to stand back and judge things.

> You're only given one point of view.

> It makes the writing more personal.

> You don't know what other people think of the writer.

> It helps you to understand the writer's feelings.

Sort the statements into advantages and disadvantages using a chart like the
one below.

Writing in the first person	
Advantages	**Disadvantages**

Writing autobiography in the second person

In the following account the writer remembers a football match. Unusually, he writes in the second person using 'you' instead of 'I'. Read the first paragraph in which the use of the second person is highlighted. Then talk about the questions that follow it.

p.205

All Points North

You were thirteen when you first went to **Old Trafford**. Being a Town fan, you'd never seen fifty thousand people gathered together in one lump, and you'd certainly never seen European football. You'd never been to a floodlit match either, and the teams came on to the pitch
5 like **Subbuteo** men tipped out on a snooker table. This was in the days before supporting Manchester United became like supporting U2 or the Sony Corporation, in the days when you handed cash over the turnstile and walked on to the terrace.

Word bank
Old Trafford – the football ground where Manchester United play their home games
Subbuteo – a table-top football game, where you flick the players with your fingers to score

---

The word 'you' is used often. Who do you think the 'you' is?
Does the use of the second person make you feel more or less involved? Explain why.
Now read on.

United were playing **Juventus**, whose goalie, Dino Zoff, was reckoned to be the best
10 in the world at the time. As he trotted out towards the **Stretford End** where you were standing, a light ripple of applause ran around the ground, and he lifted his arm and held his index finger in the air, to collect the praise and to confirm his status as the world's number one. That was his big mistake. Suddenly he was staring
15 at tens of thousands of outstretched arms, each one carrying a fist or two fingers, and the insults speared at him needed no translation into Italian. Zoff had fallen for the electric handshake. In another sense, in a split second he'd elevated himself from goalkeeper to God, and the
20 crowd were having none of it. For the rest of the match he was a troubled and lonely figure, stood as far away from the crowd as possible, only coming near to pick the ball out of the net.

Word bank
Juventus – a football team from Italy
Stretford End – the end of the pitch where the fans stand

The writer has used the second person only once, early in the paragraph.
On what or whom does he then concentrate?
Now read on.

25

30

The next round was against **Ajax**, in the days when Ajax was still pronounced like a bathroom cleaner. You were in the **Scoreboard End**. Before the kick-off, a man behind you leant over the barrier and spat a hot wet blob of bubble gum into your hair. Your friend's dad told you to leave it alone, but you messed with it for ninety minutes, and when you got back, you had to have a bald patch hacked into the top of your head to get rid of the **chuddie**. At school next day, you got battered for saying where you'd been, and battered again for looking like a medieval monk. You can't remember the score, but the net outcome was a defeat.

*from **All Points North** by Simon Armitage*

Word bank
Ajax – a Dutch football team
Scoreboard End – the end of the pitch where the scoreboard is
chuddie – muck

How many times does the writer use 'you' or 'your' in the third paragraph?
In what way does the writer move from a general experience in the second paragraph to a very personal one in the third?
Who do you think 'you' is in this paragraph?

Look back at the whole extract. Talk about the advantages and disadvantages of writing autobiography in the second person. List the main points. You could make a chart like the one you used in Activity 3.

Writing autobiography in the third person

In her autobiography *Lark Rise to Candleford* Flora Thompson writes about life in a small Oxfordshire village in the late nineteenth century. She calls herself Laura and writes in the third person, as though Laura were someone else. In the following paragraph she tells about her problems at school. The annotations show you how the third person is being used.

Refers to herself as though she were another person. — It was not until she reached Standard 1 that her troubles really began. Arithmetic was the subject by which the pupils were placed, and — Is able to stand back and look at things from a distance.

Gives herself a clear identity through the name. — as Laura could not grasp the simplest rule with such help as the mistress had time to give, she did not even know how to begin working out the sums and was permanently at the bottom of the class. — Is able to look at the problem in an impersonal way.

from **Lark Rise to Candleford** *by Flora Thompson*

Activity 4

1 Think about the examples you have read of writing in the first person (I, we), the second person (you) and the third person (he, she, it, they). Copy and complete these sentences.

> The use of the .... person allows the writer to describe events from a distance, rather like a TV camera.
> The use of the .... person allows the writer to involve the reader directly.
> The use of the .... person allows the writer to show his/her personal feelings and emotions.

2 Now experiment with writing in the second and third person. The text below begins a first person account about starting school. Read it carefully.

> It was my first day at school. I walked nervously through the school gates and looked around me. There were hundreds of pupils, much bigger than me, and they all looked as though they knew what they were doing. I felt awkward in my new uniform. My shirt collar was scratching my neck and Mum had tightened my tie so hard I thought I would choke.

    a Rewrite this text in the second person. Your opening sentence is:
       It was your first day at school.

    b Rewrite this text in the third person. Your opening sentence is:
       It was John's first day at school. (You can use your own name here.)

    c Now look at all three versions of the same text. Place a star beside the one you like the most and write the reason(s) for your choice.

Appreciating social and historical detail

From reading autobiography we can learn about:

◆ the lives of other people
◆ their customs and traditions
◆ the times in which they lived.

Activity 5 ICT WS

In the next extract, also from *Lark Rise to Candleford*, the writer creates a clear picture of a meal by giving many details. Identify these details by using a chart like the one below and making notes under the headings.

Content of the meal	How the meal was prepared	How the table was organised	Behaviour at the table

A good dinner

Here, then, were the three chief ingredients of the one hot meal a day, bacon from the **flitch**, vegetables from the garden, and flour for the roly-poly. This meal, called 'tea', was taken in the evening, when the men were home from the fields and the children from school.

5   About four o'clock, smoke would go up from the chimneys, as the fire was made up and the big iron boiler, or the three-legged pot, was slung on the hook of the chimney-chain. Everything was cooked in the one utensil; the square of bacon, amounting to little more than a taste each; cabbage, or other green vegetables in one net, potatoes in another, and the roly-poly swathed in 10 a cloth. It sounds a haphazard method in these days of gas and electric cookers; but, by carefully timing the putting in of each item and keeping the simmering of the pot well regulated, each item was kept intact and an appetising meal was produced. The water in which the food had been cooked, the potato **parings**, and other vegetable trimmings were the pig's share.

15   When the men came home from work they would find the table spread with a clean whitey-brown cloth, upon which would be knives and two-pronged steel forks. The vegetables would then be turned out into big round yellow crockery dishes and the bacon cut into dice, with much the largest cube upon **Feyther's** plate, and the whole family would sit down to the chief meal of the
20 day. True, it was seldom that all could find places at the central table; but some of the smaller children could sit upon stools with the seat of a chair for a table, or on the doorstep with their plates on their laps.

   Good manners prevailed. The children were given their share of the food, there was no picking and choosing, and they were expected to eat it in silence.
25 'Please' and 'Thank you' were permitted, but nothing more. Father and Mother might talk if they wanted to; but usually they were content to concentrate upon their
30 enjoyment of the meal.

*adapted from **Lark Rise to Candleford** by Flora Thompson*

Word bank
flitch – a side of pork salted and cured
parings – peelings
Feyther's – the writer's spelling of 'Father's' to show how they pronounced it

Activity 6 WS

1 In order to assess the detail you have noted, you need to draw on your own experience. What do you consider to be a typical family meal of today? Describe it in detail, using the same headings as in your chart in Activity 5.

2 Your notes should help you to see some similarities and differences between life in the late nineteenth century and today. Highlight these with colours or number them.

3 Use your highlighted notes to help you complete a chart like the one below. Some examples are given to start you off.

Similarities and differences between life in the 1880s and today	Evidence
They had a smaller range of food.	They had: bacon, vegetables and flour as their main ingredients. We have: …
They cooked in a different way.	They cooked on fires. We have: …
Food tasted good then and does now.	An 'appetising meal'.

Thinking about how feelings are revealed

Writers will sometimes write about painful memories. In the extract on page 88, Roald Dahl recalls a plane crash in which he was badly injured and temporarily blinded. He remembers what happened in exact detail.

Activity 7 ICT

As you are reading, place the following notes on the events in the correct sequence.

1 Heard the starboard petrol tank explode.
2 Kept dragging himself into the cooler side.
3 Rolled out head first on to the sand.
4 Heard machine-gun ammunition exploding.
5 Undid seat straps and parachute straps.
6 The plane crashed.
7 Started to drag himself away.
8 There was tremendous heat.

Using a chart like the one below, match the following phrases, which describe what Dahl was feeling, to the events.

a 'All I wanted was to go ... to sleep'
b 'great difficulty'
c 'desperate effort'
d 'I felt no pain'
e 'that didn't worry me'
f 'I was unconscious'
g 'wanted to lie down and doze off'
h 'All I wanted was to get away'
i 'enormous effort'

5							
e							

Going Solo

It is odd that I can remember very clearly quite a few of the things that followed seconds after the crash. Obviously I was unconscious for some moments, but I must have recovered my senses very quickly because I can remember hearing a mighty *whoosh* as the petrol tank in the port wing

5   exploded, followed almost at once by another mighty *whoosh* as the starboard tank went up in flames. I could see nothing at all, and I felt no pain. All I wanted was to go gently off to sleep and to hell with the flames. But soon a tremendous heat around my legs **galvanised** my soggy brain into action. With great difficulty I managed to undo first my seat-straps and then the straps of

10 my parachute, and I can even remember the desperate effort it took to push myself upright in the cockpit and roll out head first on to the sand below. Again I wanted to lie down and doze off, but the heat close by was terrific and had I stayed where I was I should simply have been roasted alive.

15 I began very very slowly to drag myself away from the awful hotness. I heard my machine-gun ammunition exploding in the flames and the bullets were pinging about all over the place but that didn't worry me. All I wanted was to get away from the tremendous heat and rest in

20 peace. The world about me was divided sharply down the middle into two halves. Both of these halves were pitch black, but one was scorching hot and the other was not. I had to keep on dragging myself away from the scorching-hot side and into the cooler one, and this took a long

25 time and enormous effort, but in the end the temperature all around me became bearable. When that happened I collapsed and went to sleep.

from Going Solo by Roald Dahl

Word bank
galvanised – moved to take action

Activity 8

1   As Dahl recounts this incident, in which he was badly burned, he keeps referring to the fire and heat but in different ways. Pick out and list as many references as you can find to fire and heat. Here are the first two.

   ◆ *in flames* (line 6)
   ◆ *to hell with the flames* (line 7)

   You should find at least eight.

2   What do these details show you about Dahl's feelings when he recounted this incident many years after it happened?

Dahl shows us the conflict between what he wants to do and what he knows he must do in order to survive by balancing the ideas. To do this he makes great use of the word 'but'. Read the following sentence.

Again I wanted to lie down and doze off	**but**	the heat close by was terrific and had I stayed where I was I should simply have been roasted alive.

Dahl could have said this in a number of different ways by using slightly different words and punctuation. Read the three sentences below closely. Identify the differences in each one.

Even though I wanted to lie down and doze off	,	the heat close by was terrific and had I stayed where I was I should simply have been roasted alive.
Again I wanted to lie down down and doze off	.	Nevertheless, the heat close by was terrific and had I stayed where I was I should simply have been roasted alive.
Again I wanted to lie down down and doze off	.	However, the heat close by was terrific and had I stayed where I was I should simply have been roasted alive.

Activity 9

1 Find three other examples of sentences in which Dahl balances the choices around the word 'but'. Write these down.

2 Choose one of the three sentences. Experiment with writing it in different ways. Use the example above to help you.

3 Why do you think Dahl chose the same sentence structure each time?

Reviewing your reading skills

Look back at the list of autobiographies you made at the start of this unit. Add to it the titles and authors of autobiographies named in this unit. Of the four you have read extracts from, which would you be most interested in reading? Why? Place the four in order of preference and aim to read your first choice.

This unit will help you to:

◆ see the link between content, purpose and audience
◆ understand how presentation affects the reader
◆ think about how media texts are influenced by readers
◆ evaluate the effectiveness of a media text.

The media and advertising

'The media' is the name given to types of communication that reach large numbers of people. Revise what you know about the media by mapping your knowledge. Think about type, content, purpose and audience. You could make notes in the form of a spidergram.

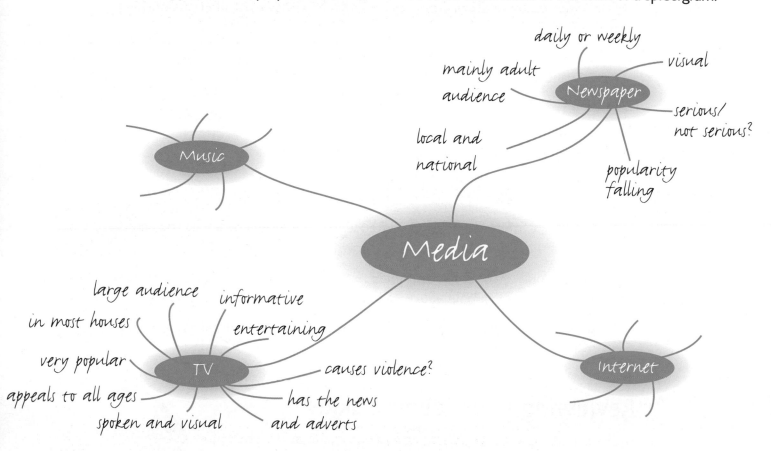

The media have the ability to reach large numbers of people in a short time. It is not surprising, therefore, that advertising often appears in the media. There are many different types of advertisements and ways of advertising.

Activity 1 ⓌⓈ

1 Read the adverts at the bottom of the page, then copy the chart below. Complete the second column of the chart by identifying the main features of each advert (the first one has been done for you). You could choose words or phrases from this list.

◆ informative	◆ bold	◆ colourful	◆ eye-catching	◆ factual
◆ chatty	◆ slang	◆ adjectives	◆ directives	
◆ persuasive	◆ lively	◆ to the point	◆ exaggerated	

2 Now decide where you might find each of the adverts, and complete the third column of the chart. Again, the first one has been done for you.

Advert	Main features of advert	Where you might find it
A	Short, informative, factual, to the point	'For Sale' section of a local newspaper
B		

A ARTICLES FOR SALE

SONY D-191
Discman, digital volume, earphones, AC power adaptor, silver, slim design, perfect working order   only £70
Tel (0736) 629581

B

'… and that's tomorrow night, don't forget, for the hottest music in town, get down to the Riverside Café and meet a host of celebs plus your very own favourite DJ …'

C

for sale

for sale

D

Spot check

E

WDCS
reg charity no: 1014705

The global voice for the protection of whales, dolphins and their environment

working on campaigns & projects in over 25 countries

When it comes to beating spots, acne or other sk… or sticks only touch the surface. The secret of … complexion goes deeper than that.

Clear Complexion tablets contain natural active herbs that help to treat your skin from within. So your skin stays clear of spots - even under close inspection! Available from Boots, Superdrug, large Tesco and Asda stores, Holland and Barrett, health shops and pharmacies.

CLEAR COMPLEXION

Linking content to purpose and audience

Every advert has the following.

---

1 **A purpose** This is the reason for which it was made. It could be to:

◆ sell a product
◆ remind the reader of a brand name ('brand awareness')
◆ persuade the reader to act or think in a particular way.

---

2 **An audience** These are the people the advertiser is hoping to influence. They are sometimes called 'consumers'. You can often work out the audience's:

◆ age
◆ gender (male/female)
◆ interests and/or needs.

Advertisements usually contains clues that help you to work out **purpose** and **audience**. Look again at the text of advert A:

Activity 2 ⓦⓢ

Copy and complete the chart below by identifying the purpose(s) and audience(s) of adverts B to E.

Advert	What you learn about the purpose(s)	What you learn about the audience(s)
A	To sell the discman To inform reader about it To persuade reader to buy it	Readers of the newspaper Teens/early twenties Interested in music Looking for a bargain
B		

The effect of presentation

Advertisers must attract and keep their audience's attention *and* get across their message. The visual impact of an advert is important as well as the language. When assessing an advert, think about:

- ◆ first impressions
- ◆ the effects of words
- ◆ the illustrations
- ◆ use of fonts
- ◆ use of colour
- ◆ layout.

Activity 3 ICT

Read the following tour advert closely. To help you assess the presentation, note your answers to the questions that surround it. Your notes can be abbreviated.

First impressions

- ◆ What do you first notice when you look at this advert?
- ◆ Choose one or two words to sum up your first impression.
- ◆ What are the purpose(s) of this advert?
- ◆ Who would this advert appeal to?
- ◆ Who would be likely to book the tours?

The effects of words

- ◆ Where is the word 'adventure'? What does it suggest?
- ◆ Where is the word 'unique'? What does it suggest?
- ◆ Why might the London Tourist Board logo be included?

The illustrations

- ◆ What are you shown in the pictures?
- ◆ What is suggested by the cartoon frog?

Use of fonts

- ◆ What use is made of different fonts (lettering)?

Use of colour

- ◆ What can you say about the use of colour?
- ◆ Why is it mostly blue?

Layout

- ◆ What is unusual about the shape?
- ◆ How is the material organised?

Activity 4 ICT WS

You are going to use your notes to help you answer the following question.

> *How does the presentation of the material in the Frog Tours advertisement target children?*

Read through all the steps of how to answer this question before starting to write.

Step 1: Look through your notes. Decide which of these will help you to answer the question. Highlight them.

Step 2: Think about how you will organise your notes into paragraphs. You could:

◆ start by writing about first impressions
◆ describe the main features of presentation that target children
◆ say whether you think the advertisement would appeal to children and why.

Step 3: Colour-code your notes to show the details you want to include in each paragraph.

Step 4: Before you start to write, read these opening sentences. The annotations highlight the features of the writing for you. You can use these sentences as your opening.

Opens with a statement, making clear what the paragraph is about.

When I first looked at the Frog Tours advertisement I could see that it was aimed at children. In order to attract children's attention it has a funny cartoon figure of a frog and uses bright, lively colours. It also …

Uses a formal tone.

Mainly written in the present tense.

Refers to features and/or details of the text to support points.

Step 5: Remember to connect your ideas clearly. Here are some useful connecting words and phrases.

◆ nex
◆ furthermore
◆ also
◆ this shows that
◆ it suggests
◆ however
◆ seems to be
◆ gives the impression
◆ so as to

When you have finished, read your answer carefully. Check that you have:

◆ included all the details you colour-coded
◆ used the features of writing highlighted in Step 4.

Responding to advertising

Advertising affects people. It affects what they buy, how they feel, how they think, who they vote for and which charities they support. It is because advertising works that companies invest huge amounts of money in it. If it didn't work, they wouldn't bother. Advertisers aim to touch people's feelings. If they can make us feel something, then we tend to take more notice.

Activity 5 ICT

Read the advert headlines. Decide which feeling the advertiser is trying to affect. Choose a suitable word from the list below. Explain your choices to a partner.

| ◆ insecurity | ◆ pity | ◆ fear | ◆ taste | ◆ greed |

WATCH OUT! There's a thief about!

Having a **BAD HAIR DAY?**

YOU TOO CAN BE A MILLIONAIRE!

This tiny kitten was brutally beaten and left to die.

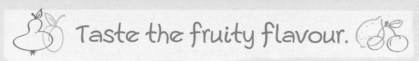

Taste the fruity flavour.

How the media is influenced

Just as advertisements influence the reader, so the reader can influence the content of the advertisement. In the following extract from its website, Barnardo's, a children's charity, explains the thinking behind its new campaign.

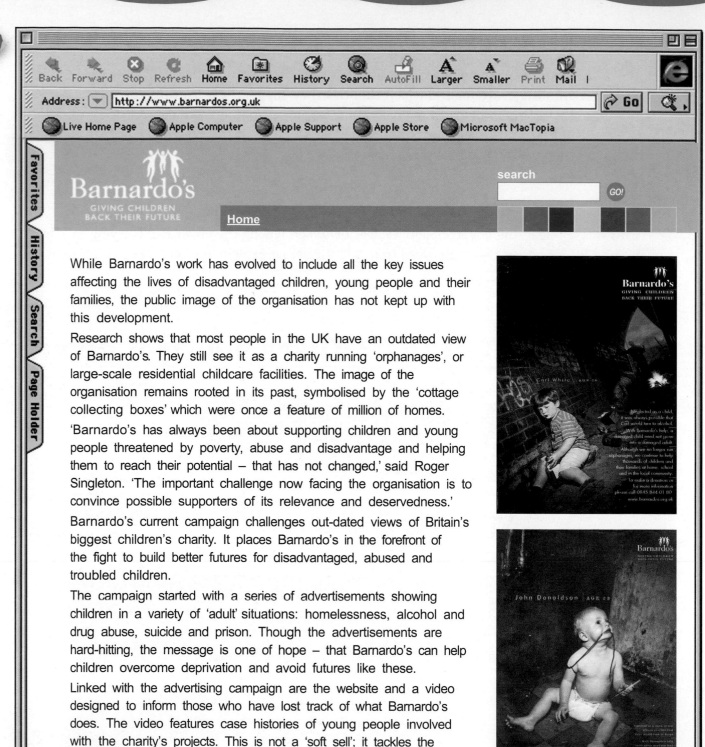

While Barnardo's work has evolved to include all the key issues affecting the lives of disadvantaged children, young people and their families, the public image of the organisation has not kept up with this development.

Research shows that most people in the UK have an outdated view of Barnardo's. They still see it as a charity running 'orphanages', or large-scale residential childcare facilities. The image of the organisation remains rooted in its past, symbolised by the 'cottage collecting boxes' which were once a feature of million of homes.

'Barnardo's has always been about supporting children and young people threatened by poverty, abuse and disadvantage and helping them to reach their potential – that has not changed,' said Roger Singleton. 'The important challenge now facing the organisation is to convince possible supporters of its relevance and deservedness.'

Barnardo's current campaign challenges out-dated views of Britain's biggest children's charity. It places Barnardo's in the forefront of the fight to build better futures for disadvantaged, abused and troubled children.

The campaign started with a series of advertisements showing children in a variety of 'adult' situations: homelessness, alcohol and drug abuse, suicide and prison. Though the advertisements are hard-hitting, the message is one of hope – that Barnardo's can help children overcome deprivation and avoid futures like these.

Linked with the advertising campaign are the website and a video designed to inform those who have lost track of what Barnardo's does. The video features case histories of young people involved with the charity's projects. This is not a 'soft sell'; it tackles the challenging and topical issues of teenage pregnancy and child sexual abuse.

*from the **Barnardo's** website*

Activity 6

1 As you read the Barnardo's advert, identify:
  ◆ the reasons why it wants to change its image
  ◆ the ways in which it is trying to change its image.

2 The campaign is described as 'hard-hitting' and 'not a "soft sell"'.
  ◆ Write your own definition of each term and check it against a partner's.
  ◆ Talk about how these terms apply to adverts you know.

Using the same text in different media

Websites often carry advertising material, as shown in the Barnardo's example opposite. Think about the way advertising on a website is similar to and/or different from advertising in a magazine or newspaper. Working with a partner, map your thoughts on this. Here are some prompts to get you started.

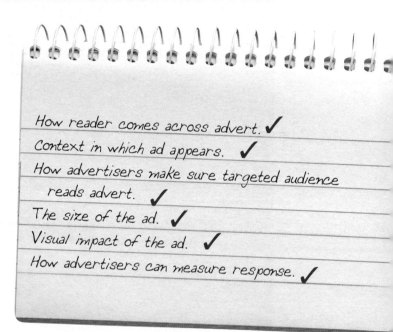

How reader comes across advert. ✔
Context in which ad appears. ✔
How advertisers make sure targeted audience reads advert. ✔
The size of the ad. ✔
Visual impact of the ad. ✔
How advertisers can measure response. ✔

Activity 7 ICT WS

Now compare the advertisement on page 98 with the extract from the website on page 96.

Copy the chart below to help you make your comparison. One feature has already been done for you. You should think of at least three others and add these to your chart.

Feature	Website	Poster
Amount of text	Lots of close text – people would need to be interested and take time to read it.	Very little text. This helps to draw attention to the impact of the photograph.

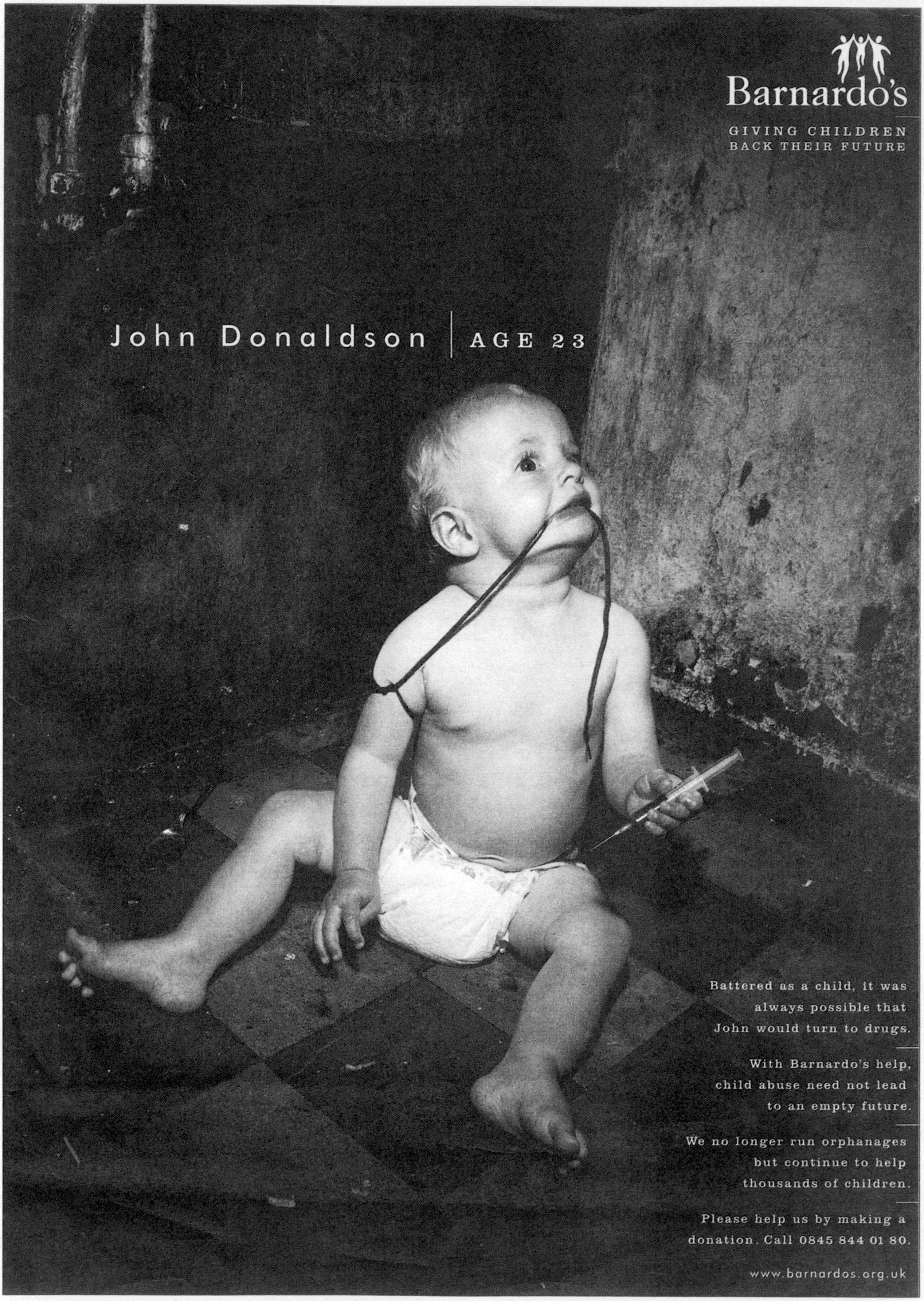

Barnardo's
GIVING CHILDREN
BACK THEIR FUTURE

John Donaldson | AGE 23

Battered as a child, it was
always possible that
John would turn to drugs.

With Barnardo's help,
child abuse need not lead
to an empty future.

We no longer run orphanages
but continue to help
thousands of children.

Please help us by making a
donation. Call 0845 844 01 80.

www.barnardos.org.uk

Writing about advertisements

When you read advertisements you are reading images as well as print. You need to interpret both in order to write about content and effectiveness.

Activity 8 ⬥WS

Study the Barnardo's advert closely. With a partner, copy and complete this chart to help you assess the advert's content and effectiveness.

Areas to consider	Barnardo's advert
First impressions	
◆ What do you notice/think/feel when you first look at the advert?	
Intended purpose(s)	
◆ What is the advert trying to do? ◆ Why do you think this?	
Intended audience(s)	
◆ Who is the advert aimed at? ◆ Why do you think this?	
Features of presentation	
◆ What can you say about the: – illustrations? – use of fonts? – use of colour? – layout?	
Interesting uses of words	
◆ How many times does the word 'Barnardo's' appear? What is the effect of this repetition? ◆ What message does the slogan give? ◆ Why do the words 'John Donaldson Age 23' appear above the picture?	
The overall effectiveness	
◆ How do the picture and words make you feel? What is the advert's message? Is it an effective advert? ◆ Give your reasons.	

11 Recognising bias

This unit will help you to:
- ◆ separate fact and opinion
- ◆ distinguish between objectivity and bias
- ◆ examine bias in detail
- ◆ identify how language is used to reinforce bias.

Separating fact and opinion

The following statements are facts.

> **There are seven days in a week.**
> **There are twelve months in a year.**

A fact is a statement that can be shown to be true.

The following statements are opinions.

> **Saturday is the best day of the week.**
> **The weather in August is better than in May.**

An opinion is a point of view. You might agree with it or disagree with it. Notice how opinions can be stated as facts.

Activity 1 🔘

Read the following passage. Identify and list the four facts and three opinions in it.

There are twenty-four hours in a day. In England the hours of daylight change depending on the time of year. Summer is the best season for many reasons. There is more sunshine and it's better to be warm than cold. Also it stays light for longer which means you can have more fun with friends.

You will also come across 'false facts' such as the following.

> **Tuesday is the first day of the week.**
> **There are thirteen months in a year.**

These are false statements, given as if correct.

Activity 2 ⓌⓈ

1 Copy and complete the following chart by sorting the statements below.

Facts	Opinions	False facts

a There are 22 hours in a day.

b Mornings are more fun than evenings.

c There are 60 minutes in an hour.

d The sun sets in the morning.

e There are three months that start with the letter 'J'.

f 3 p.m. is the worst time of day.

g 1600 hours is the same as 4 p.m.

h The month of August is named after the Roman Emperor Augustus.

i It's nicer to be born in summer than in winter.

j The sun rises in the north and sets in the south.

2 Add three examples of your own to each of the columns.

Finding out about bias

When a person is biased, he or she allows personal feelings to influence judgement. Look at the picture below and at what the people are saying. Read the annotations to understand what they are really saying.

When someone is biased he (or she) gives a one-sided view. He does not look at something from different points of view. He uses his feelings to influence his judgements.

Looking at bias and objectivity

A biased point of view is one-sided. An objective point of view is not influenced by feelings. A person with an objective point of view sees things in a more balanced way.

The following three people have different views about the same school. Read their views carefully. As you are reading, decide which is the most balanced and fair view of the school.

Mr Johnston

Well it's the most popular school in the area and all the parents want their children to go there. You have to put your child's name on a list and they don't all get accepted. Both of mine came here and they did well. The exam results are always good and they have excellent sport and drama facilities. You can tell the pupils are happy just by looking at them. It's obvious they enjoy going to school and there's never any problems with bullying or anything like that.

Amandeep

I'm very keen on sport so when I first came to look round here I really liked the look of the sports facilities. The sports field is huge and the indoor gym is very well equipped. Sport aside, we generally get quite a good education here, though some subjects are better than others. I think some of the teachers are too strict. In some lessons we have to sit in boy/girl order when I'd much rather sit with my friends. It's supposed to help you work and, to be fair, not many people misbehave in those lessons.

Tina

My Dad was really keen for me to come to this school because he used to but I wish I'd gone to a different one with my friends. If my parents would let me move to another one I'd go tomorrow. You never learn anything here. All the teachers want you to do is sit in straight rows and be quiet, while they get on with their marking. They're really strict and won't even let you sit next to your friends. They always pick on me and send me out of the class or give me extra work. It's not fair. They never pick on anyone else.

You will have noticed that both Mr Johnston and Tina give unbalanced views. Mr Johnston gives the impression that everything is wonderful and Tina talks as though everything is terrible. They are both biased. They are letting their feelings influence their judgement. Amandeep, however, weighs up the good and bad points. Of the three of them, he is being the most objective.

Activity 3

1 Add another two sentences to each of the views of Mr Johnston, Amandeep and Tina. Aim to continue the bias or the objectivity.

2 Work in pairs to review your work. Read your sentences aloud and ask your partner to:

 ◆ identify which person is speaking in each
 ◆ say why he/she thinks this.

Bias based on fact

You have seen that bias is often shown in people's opinions. Sometimes, however, it can seem to be based on facts. The bias is created by:

 ◆ the way the facts are selected
 ◆ the way the facts are used.

Read this fact file on Samantha Jones.

NAME: Samantha Jones

AGE: 34

FAMILY: husband, Lee; two children, Lisa (5) and Katy (2)

EDUCATION: to GCSE level (French D, English C, Maths C, Geography C, Science D, Food Technology C)

EMPLOYMENT: three mornings and two evenings a week as aerobics instructor at the local leisure centre

INTERESTS: keeping fit, singing with a local choir, going dancing with friends

HOME: three-bedroom first-floor flat in Manor Park Lane

Here is one account of Samantha, using details from the fact file. It has been annotated to show you how the bias is created.

Makes it seem as though this is all that matters to her.

Leaves out her other successes to make her seem less intelligent.

The use of 'sadly' and 'cheerfully' makes Samantha seem heartless.

Mother of two, Sammy Jones, likes nothing better than to go dancing with her 'friends' on a Saturday night. Fitness freak Sammy, who left school with a GCSE in cookery, likes to keep in trim shape for her nights on the town. When she's not out dancing she's doing the aerobics classes at the local leisure centre. Meanwhile little Lisa (5) can only wave sadly goodbye as her mother cheerfully leaves her in their first floor flat with baby sister Katy, aged 2.

The use of inverted commas suggests these may not just be girl friends.

The word 'freak' suggests her interest is not normal.

This distorts the facts to imply she's only bothered about herself.

Activity 4 ICT

Now read the following different account of Samantha, also based on the fact file on page 103. As you read it talk about:

◆ the impression it gives of Samantha
◆ which facts have been selected
◆ how the facts have been used to create bias.

Samantha Jones was keen to return to work once her children, Lisa (5) and Katy (2), were old enough to be looked after by their Dad, Lee. Samantha, who lives in a spacious apartment in Manor Park Lane, left school with a string of GCSEs. Always a health and fitness fanatic, she trained as an aerobics instructor and has recently joined the highly qualified staff at the Leisure Centre. When she's not keeping fit, our Mum of the Month is singing her heart out with the local church choir.

Notice how bias can be positive, selecting one set of facts to create a good impression, or negative, selecting a different set of facts to create a bad impression.

Activity 5 ICT

Read this fact file.

Name: Nicholas James Smith

Age: 16

Family: dad, Mike, and sister Beth, aged 11

Education: studying for nine GCSEs at Carlton College Comprehensive School

Employment: part-time Saturdays and Wednesday evenings, stacking shelves at the local supermarket

Interests: playing drums with local band, plays football every Sunday, girlfriend Lucy

Home: three-bedroom semi in Howton Rd

Here are some statements about Nicholas, based on the fact file. Which statements demonstrate:

◆ positive bias?   ◆ negative bias?

Write the number of the statement and explain why you think it is positive or negative.

1 He attends Carlton College, where he hopes to achieve success in nine GCSE subjects.

2 Raised in a one-parent family, he plays drums in a rock band.

3 Nick has little time for schoolwork as he prefers to stack shelves in the local supermarket.

4 Although he is only 16, his life is full and varied.

5 He maintains a high level of fitness by regularly playing football.

6 When he has some free time he pops into the local Comp, in the hope of getting a few GCSEs.

7 Though only 16 years old, Nicholas is keen to raise some extra money to help out his dad.

8 Dad, Mike, is bringing up Nicholas and his younger sister, Beth (aged 11), on his own.

9 Already Nick is sinking into the typical lads' routine of Sunday morning footy.

Identifying bias in language

Newspapers often claim to be objective in their reporting but a close examination of headlines shows this is not always so. Read this headline and decide what you think it means.

MAD WORLD WHERE CELEBS CASH IN

Notice how the use of the word 'mad' suggests foolishness and insanity. 'Cash' suggests something to do with money. 'Cash in' is a slang term meaning 'to take advantage of'. By using 'mad' and 'cash in' the writer shows that he doesn't approve of the amount of money celebrities are getting. Through the headline the writer is trying to influence the way readers think before they read the article. When words are used in this way they are sometimes said to be 'loaded'.

Activity 6 ⓦⓢ

Read the following headlines in which the writers make their views clear by their choice of words. For each one identify:

◆ what the headline means

◆ which words are loaded

◆ how these words show the point of view.

An example has been done for you.

This shows me that the writer thinks this is very bad – a disgrace.

Home is a place where you should feel happy and safe, so the link with 'heartbreak' is unexpected.

BABY SCANDAL OF HEARTBREAK HOMES

This word suggests something very sad and upsetting.

1   ## Frail and elderly suffer in a sick society

2   ## BOYS IN CRISIS NOW

3   ## Super Soccer Star Scores Again

Examining bias in images

Bias is found not only in newspaper headlines but also in reports and articles.

Look at these photographs:

Photograph A   **Photograph B**

Activity 7 ⓦⓢ

Working in pairs, talk with a partner about your impressions of the two men in the photographs. Record your ideas on a chart like this.

	Photograph A	Photograph B	Similar/ Different?
Angle and distance of camera shot			
Facial expressions			
Clothes			
Background detail			

Now read these descriptions.

NAME:	Andrew Bennett
AGE:	59
STATUS:	Member of Parliament and former teacher
HOME:	Semi-detached house in Heaton in Mersey
INCOME:	£43,000
MANNER:	Concerned intellectual
HOBBIES:	Rambling

NAME:	Nicholas van Hoogstraten
AGE:	53
STATUS:	Landowner and property magnate
HOME:	Building Britain's biggest private house – £30m of it
INCOME:	Unknown, estate valued at £200m
MANNER:	Arrogant in the extreme
HOBBIES:	Wealth

Activity 8

1 The writer presents these descriptions as fact files. Is she right to do so? Decide:
   - ◆ which details are factual
   - ◆ which details are not factual
   - ◆ what impressions these facts give
   - ◆ what impressions these details give.

2 Which description would you match to:
   - ◆ photograph A?
   - ◆ photograph B?

   Give at least two reasons for your choice.

Developing your understanding of bias

As you have seen, bias can be negative or positive and can be used to influence the reader into supporting a particular idea or point of view. Below you will find the article from which the pictures and 'fact files' were taken. Now read the full article.

Van Hoogstraten

Bennett

Word bank

irreconcilable – cannot reach agreement

ramblers – people who enjoy walking in the countryside

trespass – to go on to someone's property without permission

Rumble in the Countryside

For years they have been two **irreconcilable** forces – **ramblers** who believe they have the right to roam and wealthy landlords who believe they do not. The ramblers have staged much-celebrated mass **trespasses** and the landlords in return have set loose the dogs.

The bitterness and the great social divide have rarely been better brought to life than in the amazing conflict involving one of Stockport's MPs and one of the country's richest men.

In the red corner stands Andrew Bennett, Labour MP for Reddish, President of the Ramblers Association and noble protector of Britain's humble public footpaths.

In the true blue corner is Nicholas van Hoogstraten. Multi-millionaire property owner. The man who refers to ramblers in frightening Nazi-speak as 'the great unwashed'. He is not a man to forgive those who trespass against him.

The battle began last week when Andrew Bennett, a lifelong and committed rambler, led a demonstration at Van Hoogstraten's High Cross estate in East Sussex because the property tycoon and former slum landlord had blocked an ancient footpath that runs through his land.

Two more contrasting men there could not be.

Mr Van Hoogstraten was a millionaire by the time he was 23 who owned 350 properties in Sussex alone. These days he is building a huge £30 million palace on his High Cross estate. It will be Britain's biggest private house.

And when he decided he wanted privacy, a lowly footpath was not going to get in his way. Explaining why he had surrounded the right of way with barbed wire, he declared: 'The only purpose in creating wealth like mine is to separate oneself from the riff-raff.'

How wrong he was.

Mr Bennett and the Ramblers Association were immediately on the war path. They made High Cross a target in their campaign to open up all rights of way.

Speaking after the demonstration, Bennett told the *Stockport Express*: 'The network of public footpaths belongs to everyone and is part of our history. Walking the country is something everyone is entitled to and we will protect this right.'

Is it worth what is going to be a lengthy and expensive battle? It is only one bit of footpath in the country. But the right to roam will be something of the past if Van Hoogstraten is allowed to win. Andrew Bennett can only hope the matter is taken up in parliament.

One thing is for sure, he won't give up.

*adapted from 'Rumble in the Countryside' in **The Stockport Express***

Activity 9 ICT WS

1 Scan the article to identify the new details you are given about Andrew Bennett and Nicholas van Hoogstraten. List them in a chart like the one below:

Andrew Bennett	Nicholas van Hoogstraten

Read through the details you have listed. Place the letter 'F' beside each fact in your list.

2 Write down what each man is quoted as saying. What do these quotations make you think about each man?

3 Look at your answers to 1 and 2. What do these details tell you about:

◆ what the writer thinks of each man?
◆ the impression she wants to give the reader?

Finding out how words can show bias

Writers often use words to emphasise their point of view.

Andrew Bennett is described as a 'lifelong and committed rambler'. The word 'lifelong' shows that this is not just a fad. This is emphasised by the word 'committed', which suggests dedication and loyalty. These are positive qualities.

Nicholas van Hoogstraten is described as the 'property tycoon and former slum landlord'. 'Property tycoon' and 'slum landlord' are placed next to each other to emphasise that, although he is very wealthy, the properties he rents are not well cared for. The word 'slum' suggests something unpleasant and sleazy about him. These are negative qualities.

In both cases the writer is using words to give a particular impression.

Activity 10 (WS)

1 Here are two other examples of words being used to emphasise point of view:

Andrew Bennett: 'noble protector of Britain's humble public footpaths'

Van Hoogstraten: 'The man who refers to ramblers in frightening Nazi-speak as "the great unwashed".'

Highlight the important words in each example and explain the effects they have.

2 Throughout the article the writer uses the language of conflict; for example we are told that 'The battle began last week'. One reason why she does this is to make it sound more exciting. List at least four more examples of this language of conflict.

3 Work out how you found your four examples for question 2 by answering these questions.

◆ What kind of reading did you use? Was it skimming, scanning or close reading?

◆ What clues did you look for?

◆ How did you decide if an example was appropriate?

4 Another reason why the writer uses this language of conflict is to emphasise the differences between the two men. Using your knowledge of the text, and working with a partner, make a list of the ways in which Bennett and Van Hoogstraten are different. It will help you to think about:

◆ the kind of people they are

◆ their views on public footpaths

◆ the way they treat other people

◆ their social class or status.

RUMBLE IN THE COUNTRYSIDE

The following extract is taken from Maya Angelou's autobiography, *I Know Why The Caged Bird Sings*. In the book she describes growing up in the 1930s in Arkansas, a southern state of the United States of America.

Looking at detail

1 The Store is the setting for the extract. Copy the chart below. As you read lines 1–34 record what you find out about the Store in the mornings. Select details on:

♦ the Store's appearance and atmosphere

♦ what the people are like

♦ the kinds of things they do and say.

Record your details in the **first** column of your chart. An example has been done for you.

The Store in the mornings	The Store in the late afternoons
Lamplight – 'soft make-believe feeling'	

6 marks

W
p.204

I Know Why The Caged Bird Sings

Each year I watched the field across from the Store turn caterpillar green, then gradually frosty white. I knew exactly how long it would be before the big wagons would pull into the front yard and load on the cotton pickers at daybreak to carry them to the remains of **slavery's plantations**.

5   During the picking season my grandmother would get out of bed at four o'clock (she never used an alarm clock) and creak down to her knees and chant in a sleep-filled voice, 'Our Father, thank you for letting me see this New Day. Thank you that you didn't allow the bed I lay on last night to be my cooling board, nor my blanket my winding sheet. Guide my feet this day along the
10 straight and narrow and help me to put a bridle on my tongue. Bless this house, and everybody in it. Thank you, in the name of your Son, Jesus Christ, Amen.'

    Before she had quite arisen, she called our names and gave orders, and pushed her large feet into homemade slippers and across the bare wooden floor to light the coal-oil lamp.

15   The lamplight in the Store gave a soft make-believe feeling to our world
which made me want to whisper and walk about on tiptoe. The odors of onions
and oranges and kerosene had been mixing all night and wouldn't be disturbed
until the wooded slat was removed from the door and the early morning air
forced its way in with the bodies of people who had walked miles to reach the
20 pickup place.

    'Sister, I'll have two cans of sardines.'

    'I'm gonna work so fast today I'm gonna make you look like you standing still.'

    'Lemme have a hunk of cheese and some sody crackers.'

    'Just gimme a coupla them fat peanut paddies.' That would be from a picker
25 who was taking his lunch. The greasy brown paper sack was stuck behind the
bib of his overalls. He'd use the candy as a snack before the noon sun called the
workers to rest.

    In those tender mornings the Store was full of laughing, joking, boasting and
bragging. One man was going to pick two hundred pounds of cotton, and
30 another three hundred. Even the children were promising to bring home
fo' bits and six bits.

    The champion picker of the day before was the hero of the dawn. If he said
that the cotton on today's field was going to be sparse and stick to the bolls like
glue, every listener would grunt a hearty agreement.

35 The sound of the empty cotton sacks dragging over the floor and the
murmurs of waking people were sliced by the cash register as we rang up the
five-cent sales.

Word bank

slavery's plantation – the huge farms on which the cotton is
grown and which, not long before, had been run on slave labour

fo' bits and six bits – small amounts of money

supernatural – a magical source

white commissary – a shop supplying food and/or equipment

paranoia – intense suspicion

ws **2** In lines 38–50 the writer describes the Store in the late afternoons.
Record details in the **second** column of your chart about:

◆ the Store's appearance and atmosphere
◆ what the people are like
◆ the kinds of things they do and say.

The Store in the mornings	The Store in the late afternoons
Lamplight – 'soft make-believe feeling'	Dying sunlight

6 marks

If the morning sounds and smells were touched with **the supernatural**, the late afternoon had all the features of the
40 normal Arkansas life. In the dying sunlight the people dragged, rather than their empty cotton sacks.

Brought back to the Store, the pickers would step out of the backs of trucks and fold down, dirt-disappointed, to the ground. No matter how much they had picked, it wasn't
45 enough. Their wages wouldn't even get them out of debt to my grandmother, not to mention the huge bill that waited on them at the **white commissary** downtown.

The sounds of the new morning had been replaced with grumbles about cheating houses, weighted scales, snakes,
50 skimpy cotton and dusty rows.

In later years I was to confront the stereotyped picture of gay song-singing cotton pickers with such rage that I was told even by fellow Blacks that my **paranoia** was embarrassing. But I had seen the fingers cut by the mean little cotton bolls,
55 and I had witnessed the backs and shoulders and arms and legs resisting any further demands.

*adapted from **I Know Why The Caged Bird Sings**
by Maya Angelou*

Using notes for representing information

3 Use the notes from your chart to help you write five sentences in which you compare the Store in the morning with the Store in the late afternoon. Remember to:

◆ point out similarities and/or differences

◆ refer to the text and use quotations.

Here is an example.

In the morning the lamplight in the Store gives a 'soft make-believe feeling' whereas in the afternoon we are told the sunlight is 'dying'.

Use these words and phrases to help you make comparisons.

◆ but …	◆ on the other hand …	◆ similarly …
◆ however …	◆ in contrast …	◆ whereas …

10 marks

Thinking about language

4 In line 16 Maya Angelou refers to the 'odors' of onions and oranges. What is different about the spelling of this word? What is the reason for this difference?

2 marks

5 In lines 21–24 ('Sister,' to 'them fat peanut paddies'), Maya Angelou shows us how the cotton pickers spoke. Identify **three** ways in which their speech is different from standard English. An example has been done for you in the following chart.

Example of speech	Explanation of how it is different from standard English
sody crackers	Uses different words

6 marks

6 Re-read these lines closely:

In the dying sunlight the <u>people dragged</u>, rather than their empty cotton sacks.

Brought back to the Store, the pickers would step out of the backs of trucks and <u>fold down</u>, <u>dirt-disappointed</u>, to the ground.

Copy and complete the following chart to show you understand the effects of the underlined words.

Words used to describe the people	What is unusual about the words	The picture the words give of the people
the people <u>dragged</u>		
they would <u>fold down</u>		
they were <u>dirt-disappointed</u>		

6 marks

Examining the cultural background

7   What do you learn about the writer's culture from this passage? It will help you to think about:

   ◆ the grandmother's prayer
   ◆ the different types of food
   ◆ the things you learn about the way the cotton pickers live.   **6 marks**

Thinking about the author's point of view

8   In this passage the writer describes a scene from her childhood. In lines 51–56, however, we find out about her as an adult.

   a What is the 'stereotyped picture' she objects to?   **2 marks**

   b What does this paragraph show you about:

   ◆ how the writer feels about this stereotyped picture?
   ◆ the reasons for her feelings?
   ◆ what she is like as an adult?   **6 marks**

   TOTAL 50 marks

Section D ◆ Writing non-fiction
Introduction

Throughout Key Stages 2 and 3 you will have learned that different types of non-fiction texts have their own styles and conventions, or accepted ways of writing. You will have learned how to adapt the style and structure of non-fiction texts to suit the needs of your audience and your reasons for writing. The units in this section will extend your skills in writing for a range of purposes.

In Unit 13, *Writing to inform, describe and explain*, you will learn how to organise your information clearly and adapt your style of writing according to the needs of your readers. You will learn how to use details to make information clearer for your readers. You will also learn how to structure your ideas to explain events and ideas clearly for your readers.

In Unit 14, *Presenting a persuasive speech*, you will learn how to present a case persuasively and how to use techniques that will capture the attention of your readers.

In Unit 15, *Writing to advise*, you will learn how to offer advice in both personal and impersonal ways, how to meet objections your readers might make and how to present your advice effectively.

In Unit 16, *Writing to analyse*, you will learn how to analyse situations and texts in a logical way and present your ideas and conclusions clearly based on the available evidence.

Unit 17 tests you on the skills you will develop as you work carefully through the four units.

This unit will help you to:

◆ organise and present information clearly

◆ use descriptive detail to make accounts vivid for your readers

◆ put together and organise information from a range of sources

◆ give clear and well-organised explanations.

Organising and presenting information

Information texts usually begin with an opening statement that introduces the topic to the reader.

Read the text below, which has been written for a travel guide to New York. It has been written to provide interesting information for tourists about a well-known landmark.

The Statue of Liberty

The Statue of Liberty (a gift from the people of France to the people of America in 1886) is the statue of a
5 woman holding a torch in her right hand.

The sculptor, Frédéric Bartholi modelled the statue on a huge scale. She is 152
10 feet tall, weighs 2,225 tons and has a 35 foot waistline. Her index finger is eight feet long and even one of her fingernails is 13 inches long.

Activity 1

This text contains the following types of information:

◆ facts and figures about the Statue of Liberty ◆ shape of the statue

◆ when presented to America ◆ details about the design.

Work with a partner to put the information in the order it appears in the text. Write out the correct order.

You will notice that the **topic sentence** (the first sentence) gives the reader general information about the Statue of Liberty. You will also notice that the information becomes **more detailed** as the paragraph progresses and that the final sentence gives the **most detailed** information of all.

Looking closely at the way the text is written

Activity 2 ⬥ICT

Read the text on the Statue of Liberty again and work with a partner to choose the correct statement from the list below. Use the information box to help you make the right choice.

1 a The text is written in the first person.
  b The text is written in the third person.

2 a The text is written mainly in the past tense.
  b The text is written mainly in the present tense.

3 a The text has an informal tone using everyday vocabulary and expressions.
  b The text has a formal tone (using words that are more likely to be used in writing than in speech).

4 a The text begins with a topic sentence to introduce the subject to the reader.
  b The text begins with what someone has said about the Statue of Liberty.

5 a The text contains some facts and some opinions.
  b The text contains facts only.

Information box

◆ Past tense describes things that have already happened – was, did.
◆ Present tense describes things as they are now – is, has.
◆ First person – I, we.
◆ Third person – he, she, it, they.
◆ Facts can be proved to be true.
◆ Opinion is what someone thinks about something, his/her personal point of view.

Activity 3 ICT WS

The notes opposite are about the Taj Mahal. You are going to use them to write two to three paragraphs for a tourist guide on India.

Taj Mahal

- Built by Shah Jehan
- Built as tomb for beloved wife
- Wife died in childbirth
- Took 22 years to build, with over 20,000 workmen
- Completed 1653
- Set in gardens
- Main building with white marble dome
- Surrounded by four towers
- Stands on a red sandstone platform
- Carvings in marble
- Precious stones set in marble
- On the banks of river in the town of Agra, in India

Step 1: Organise the notes into groups using these headings.

- Importance and purpose of the Taj Mahal
- Location (place where you can find it)
- Shape of building and general features
- Details of the design
- Facts and figures about the Taj Mahal

Step 2: Decide on the order in which you will use the notes. Put a number next to each heading to show the sequence (order).

Step 3: Write your first paragraph. Think carefully about your **topic sentence** (first sentence). Remember the topic sentence introduces the subject, it does not include details. Then use the information from your notes to write the rest of the paragraph.

Step 4: Now write your second paragraph. Begin with a topic sentence that introduces the information you will use in this paragraph.

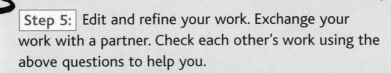

Does the account use the past tense to write about events that have taken place?

Does the account use the present tense to write about things as they are now?

Can the reader follow the organisation of ideas and work out the sequence?

Does the account sound formal avoiding the language of everyday conversation?

Step 5: Edit and refine your work. Exchange your work with a partner. Check each other's work using the above questions to help you.

Step 6: Make any alterations suggested by your partner, then write the final version.

Using descriptive detail to make accounts vivid

Read the following account of a visit to the Taj Mahal where a travel writer describes her first visit to India. This text is different from the one you have just written because this writer is giving a very personal view of her visit. She does not just include facts, she describes her feelings for her readers and includes her opinions. She also includes descriptive details to help her readers picture the scene very clearly.

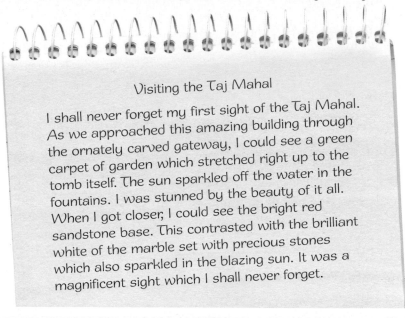

Visiting the Taj Mahal

I shall never forget my first sight of the Taj Mahal. As we approached this amazing building through the ornately carved gateway, I could see a green carpet of garden which stretched right up to the tomb itself. The sun sparkled off the water in the fountains. I was stunned by the beauty of it all. When I got closer, I could see the bright red sandstone base. This contrasted with the brilliant white of the marble set with precious stones which also sparkled in the blazing sun. It was a magnificent sight which I shall never forget.

Activity 4

1 Work with a partner to sort the following list into the order in which the text is organised.

   ◆ Writer's opinions about the Taj Mahal
   ◆ Description of first sight of the building
   ◆ Final thoughts about the experience
   ◆ Close focus on the features of the building

2 Find an example from the text of each of the features on the list above. Write down each example.

Looking closely at sentences

By using complex sentences, writers can combine several ideas in one sentence. Consider this example from the text on page 120.

Main clause.——[It was a magnificent sight] [which I shall never forget.]——Subordinate clause.

Connective.

Activity 5

1 Look at these simple sentences. They are all contained within complex sentences in the Taj Mahal text. See if you can spot the places where these sentences appear.

   ◆ I could see a green carpet of garden.
   ◆ I could see the bright red sandstone base.
   ◆ This contrasted with the brilliant white of the marble.

2 Look at the connectives in the box below. Write down the ones that are used in the Taj Mahal text.

◆ after	◆ although	◆ as	◆ because	◆ before	◆ if	
◆ once	◆ though	◆ until	◆ when	◆ where	◆ which	◆ who

3 What have you noticed about the way in which the simple sentences have been made complex?

By using complex sentences the writer can vary the style of a text. Look at this account of a trip to the Eiffel Tower written by a student who has used simple sentences only. You will see that this has made the account seem rather stilted and uninteresting to read.

A Trip to Remember
I climbed the Eiffel Tower on a Friday morning.
It was quite cold. I was a bit nervous.
   I really wanted to climb the tower. The lift was old and rusty. It was a bit like a cage. You could see out of the sides of the lift. I didn't want to look around me.

Activity 6

There are eight simple sentences in this account. These can be combined in pairs to make complex sentences, to make the text more interesting. For example:

> I climbed the Eiffel Tower on a Friday morning **when** it was quite cold.

Notice that the connective 'when' has been added to join the two sentences.

Now join the next three pairs of sentences from the student's text to form complex sentences. Use connectives from the list on page 121, or think of your own. You may need to miss out some words from the sentences when you join them together.

Adding descriptive detail

Descriptive details help your readers to imagine the scene more easily. The writer of the text about the Taj Mahal (page 120) wrote: 'I could see a green carpet of garden'. The writer could have written: 'I could see a garden', but the phrase 'green carpet of' helps the reader to imagine the scene more clearly.

How many more examples of **descriptive details** can you find in the text? Aim to find four.

Activity 7 ICT

Read the rest of the student's account of his trip to the Eiffel Tower. This is the student's first draft; he has written his ideas for improvement on the text.

Add detail here, what shows I was nervous?	I began to feel more and more nervous. At the top I dared to look around. I could see for miles.
Add details about sights on river.	I could see the River Seine with little boats on it. I could also see the roads from the tower.
Find better words to describe my feelings, describe actions to show that I was pleased.	I was pleased that I had done it.

Add more detail to show how I felt?

Need to explain what could I see/what the view was like.

Include my opinion of this view.

1 Use the student's notes to add descriptive details to the text to help readers imagine the scene more easily.

2 When you have finished, compare your work with that of a partner. Ask your partner's advice about adding even more detail, then write the final draft.

Combining and organising information from a range of sources

Sometimes writers of information texts use information they have obtained from several different places. Your next task is to study six different sources of information. You will use these sources to write a factual account of events surrounding the final voyage of the *Mary Celeste*. Begin by choosing the information from sources 1 to 6 that will be most useful for your task and make notes on it.

Activity 8 ⬥ICT

1 As you read the various sources on pages 123–124, use these headings to help you organise your notes:

> ◆ Background to the *Mary Celeste*: what was it, where was it going, who was on it
> ◆ What went wrong
> ◆ Evidence that gives clues about what went wrong

Remember: notes are brief. You do not need to write in full sentences.

2 When you have finished reading the sources, go over your notes again asking yourself these questions:

◆ Have I recorded the same information more than once?
◆ Do I have any gaps in my notes?
◆ Do I need to go back and add more information?
◆ Have I recorded information that is not relevant?

Source 1: Fact file

Name of ship:	*Mary Celeste*
Date of departure:	7 November 1872
Port of departure:	New York
Destination:	Genoa, Italy
Cargo:	1700 barrels of raw American alcohol
Captain of ship:	Captain Benjamin Briggs (aged 37); had previously captained three other ships
First mate:	Albert Richardson
Second mate:	A. Gilling
Cook:	E. W. Head
Other crew members:	V. Lorenzen, B. Lorenzen (brothers), A. Marten, G. Goodschall
Passengers:	Mrs Briggs and Sophie, wife and two-year-old daughter of Captain Briggs
The discovery:	Made on 5 December 1872 by Captain Morehouse, captain of the *Dei Gratia* on a route similar to that of the *Mary Celeste*.

Notes

◆ Sailors from the *Dei Gratia* found no sign of the *Mary Celeste's* crew.
◆ The boat appeared to be seaworthy.
◆ No trace of the crew was ever found.

Source 2: Letter from Captain Briggs to his mother

We seem to have a very good mate and Steward and I hope we shall have a pleasant journey.

Source 3: Comments to newspaper by Mrs Richardson, wife of the first mate

'I always believed and will always believe that my husband, Captain Briggs, Mrs Briggs, her baby and the cook were murdered by the crew.' Her husband, she stated, had a **presentiment** of evil before he sailed.

Word bank
presentiment – feeling that something will happen

Source 4: Statements from the Court of Enquiry

John Wright
I could not tell whether any boat had or had not been there at all. There were no davits on the quarter of the vessel. I saw nothing from which I could judge whether a boat had been upon deck. I saw no ropes on either side showing that a boat had been launched from the ship at all.

Word bank
davits – used for lowering the lifeboat

Source 5: Letter from Gibraltar's Attorney-General to the American Consul in Gibraltar

On examining the starboard topgallant rail, marks were discovered, apparently of blood, and a mark of a blow, and apparently of a sharp one. On descending through the fore-hatch, a barrel, ostensibly of alcohol, appeared to be tampered with.

Word bank
topgallant rail – the sail above the top mast sail
ostensibly – seeming to be
tampered with – interfered with

Source 6: Meteorological Report

The records of the Servicio Meterologico (weather forecasting service) in the Azores say that the weather deteriorated that morning and a storm blew up involving gale force winds and torrential rain.

Activity 9 ⓦ⑤

Write your account of the events during the voyage following these stages.

1 Number your notes in the order you intend to use them. Remember you do not have to organise your article strictly in the order that events happened.

2 Plan your ideas using a chart like the one below to help you.

Paragraph 1 Your opening statement/ what this text is about	
Paragraph 2 Organise the first section of your notes here What do you want your readers to know first?	
Paragraph 3 Organise the rest of your notes here	
Paragraph 4 What information do you want to use in your conclusion?	

3 Write your first draft. Remember to:

   ◆ use the past tense for events that took place in the past
   ◆ use dates and times to make the information precise
   ◆ keep to facts, avoid opinions.

4 When you have finished your first draft, give your work to a partner to read. Ask him/her to check that:

   ◆ he/she can understand your information easily
   ◆ your information is clear and could easily be understood by someone who knew nothing about the *Mary Celeste*.

5 Make any alterations necessary and write your final draft.

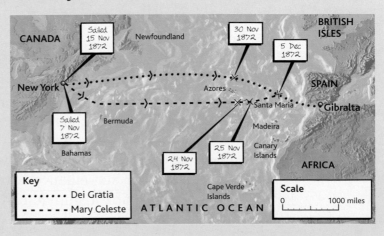

Writing to explain

Now that you have given your readers the facts about the *Mary Celeste*, you are going to write your own explanation for the disappearance of the crew. As you will remember, an **explanation** tells readers **how** and **why** things happen. It makes links for readers between **causes** and their **effects**.

Activity 10

1 Look at the explanation text below about the Bermuda Triangle. Some of the connectives have been missed out. With a partner, work out which connectives from the list below should fill in the gaps. Only use each connective once.

> ◆ because   ◆ as result of   ◆ therefore   ◆ in this way

2 Three words and one phrase have been highlighted in **bold** in the text. These are words and phrases that express possibility, they do not state that something has definitely happened. Why are words like these useful when you are giving explanations that might be true, but have not been definitely proved?

The Bermuda triangle is a region of the western Atlantic Ocean where many ships have vanished. Over the years there have been many theories put forward to explain what might cause the disappearance of ships. Firstly in this area there are many tropical storms which can build up very quickly. These storms are not always detected by satellite surveillance and so they **could** easily sink a ship quickly and without trace.

Scientists have found that there is a great deal of seismic (earthquake) activity in the area. **It is possible** that ...... this activity underwater earthquakes are causing ships and planes to disappear.

In addition, the Gulf Stream is a very strong current which **can** throw sailors off course ...... they do not know how to compensate for it....... ships **might** be destroyed in the area of the Bermuda Triangle.

When you are writing to explain you use words known as **causal connectives**. These are words that link causes and effects. For example:

Cause. ——┌ These storms are not always detected by
          │ satellite surveillance and so they could
Connective. ┘ easily sink a ship quickly and without trace. ┘ —Effect.

Activity 11

You are going to add to your information text about the *Mary Celeste* by providing readers with an explanation of what might have happened to the ship's crew. Follow these steps.

Step 1: Look back at the notes you made earlier on the *Mary Celeste*.

Step 2: Read the source material again.

Step 3: Decide which sources might provide an explanation and which are not helpful. Work with a partner to discuss your theories about the *Mary Celeste*.

Step 4: Write your explanation referring to two or three possible theories before you give your final explanation choosing the one you think is the most believable.

Step 5: Exchange your work with a partner. You should each ask the other:

◆ Does my explanation make sense?
◆ Is it believable?
◆ Have I linked my ideas clearly enough?

Step 6: Now make any alterations you think necessary before you write the final draft.

Remember to:

◆ use a topic sentence to introduce the explanation to your readers,
   e.g.: *There are many theories about the disappearance of the crew ...*
◆ use connectives, such as: *so, because, as a result of, therefore* to show the relationship between cause and effect
◆ use *could, may* and *might* with your verbs to suggest possibility (remember no one knows exactly what happened to the *Mary Celeste*)
◆ use sentence starters, such as: *It is possible that ...* or *Maybe ... .*

This unit will help you to:

◆ organise and structure your ideas when writing a speech

◆ understand how to use rhetorical devices

◆ present a case persuasively.

Planning to make an impact

When you make a speech it is very important to plan and structure your ideas so that you can make an impact on your audience.

The extract opposite is taken from a speech made by Chief Joseph, the leader of a tribe of Native Americans. His tribe, the Nez Perces, have just surrendered (given in) to the American army after long battles over who should own land. His audience for the speech is officers of the American army.

Activity 1 ICT

Read the extract. In this part of his speech, Chief Joseph accepts that he and his tribe have lost the battle.

1 Why do you think he might make a speech after his tribe have lost? What do you think was his purpose?

2 Working in pairs, answer 'true' or 'false' to each of the following statements to help you work out the purpose of the speech.

a Chief Joseph made the speech to save face in front of the Americans.

b Chief Joseph made the speech because he was angry with the Americans.

c Chief Joseph made the speech because he felt he had let his people down.

d Chief Joseph made the speech to make his defeat seem noble.

e Chief Joseph made the speech to make the American army feel guilty about what they had done to the Native Americans.

Defeat

I am tired of fighting. Our chiefs are killed. Looking Glass is dead. Toohoolhoolzote is dead. The old men are all dead. Ollokot, he who led the young men, is dead.

5 It is cold, and we have no blankets. The little children are freezing to death. My people, some of them, have run away to the hills, and have no blankets, no food. No one knows where they are – perhaps freezing to death. I want to have time to look for my children,
10 and see how many of them I can find. Maybe I shall find them among the dead.

Hear me, my chiefs! I am tired. My heart is sick and sad. From where the sun now stands I will fight no more forever.

Chief Joseph

Looking at the structure of the speech

A good speech is well structured. Chief Joseph's speech has been very clearly organised and sequenced (put in order).

Activity 2 ICT WS

1 Work with a partner to put the following notes in an order that matches the speech. This will help you to understand how the speech has been organised and how the ideas are linked together. When you have decided which is the right order, copy the chart below and sort the phrases under the headings.

- ◆ talks personally but on behalf of his tribe
- ◆ sums up the situation for the men, the fighters and the chiefs
- ◆ gives an overall view of the situation
- ◆ goes into detail about living conditions
- ◆ gives evidence to back up what he says
- ◆ the speech becomes more personal and emotional
- ◆ repeats the message

Opening	Development	Ending

2 Now think about the **content** of the three paragraphs of the speech and answer the questions on page 130.

A powerful opening

A powerful beginning is important to get your readers' attention straight away. Look again at the first sentence of Chief Joseph's speech: *I am tired of fighting*.

a Do you think this sentence would get readers' attention? Why?

b Chief Joseph says he is tired of fighting. Do you think he means:
   ◆ he can go no further and needs to sleep?
   ◆ he has had enough and does not want to fight any more?
   ◆ he can no longer bear to see the results of the fighting?

c Do you think he is speaking for himself or for his whole tribe when he describes how he feels?

Providing evidence is a good way to develop your ideas

In the middle of the speech Chief Joseph provides evidence to convince his listeners.

a What evidence does he include? Find at least three examples.

b How does this evidence prove that he is tired of fighting?

A good speech needs a memorable conclusion

At the end of his speech Chief Joseph goes back to the point he made at the beginning. What is this point?

Now plan a speech of your own, using what you have learned about structure and content. The title of your speech is:

> *Why students deserve an extra week's holiday at the end of the school year*

Your audience will be teachers and students on the school council.

Activity 3

First, think about how you will structure and sequence your speech. Look carefully at the points below. Working in pairs, decide which points should go in a powerful opening, a section where ideas are developed, and a memorable conclusion. You could use a chart like the one in Activity 2.

   ◆ We all work very hard throughout the year.
   ◆ Students deserve a reward for their hard work.
   ◆ A lot of activities take place at the end of a school year and interrupt learning, such as ...
   ◆ Year 11 students do all of their work in a shortened school year; other students could do the same.
   ◆ Nobody works well when they are tired.
   ◆ Students would work harder if the term was shorter.
   ◆ Teachers deserve a rest as well, they also work very hard.
   ◆ An extra week's holiday would encourage students to work harder.

It is important that you keep these notes as you will need them for reworking in Acivities 5, 7 and 9.

Getting the attention of your audience

Rhetorical devices are special ways of using words to persuade your audience to pay attention to your speech. You need to look at Chief Joseph's speech (page 129) in more detail to see how rhetorical devices are used. Re-read the first paragraph.

> I am tired of fighting. Our chiefs are killed. Looking Glass is dead. Toohoolhoolzote is dead. The old men are all dead. Ollokot, he who led the young men, is dead.

Activity 4 ICT WS

Find examples of rhetorical devices from this paragraph. Copy and complete the chart. Write an example from the speech of each device in the second column. In the third column match the correct phrase from the list below to describe the effect of each on the audience.

Device	Example	Effect
Short simple sentence	Our chiefs are killed.	b
Repeating key words		
Using first person pronoun to give a personal view		
Referring to individual people		

Effects

a Makes the message seem more personal.

b Helps to get message across more easily.

c Reminds audience about the message of the speech.

d Helps the audience to see things from your point of view.

Activity 5 WS

1 Look back at the plan you made in Activity 3. Write the opening of the speech in no more than three or four sentences. As you are writing, remember to:

- use short sentences for effect ◆ mention names of individual people
- explain your own feelings using the first person pronoun 'I' ◆ repeat key words.

Include the following words to help you describe your feelings.

> ◆ hard   ◆ stressful   ◆ tired   ◆ deserve

2 When you have finished, read your work aloud to a friend, then show him/her your paragraph. Ask if he/she can spot the rhetorical devices you have used.

Adding to your knowledge of rhetorical devices

Once you have grabbed the attention of your audience, you should develop your ideas in more detail, continuing to use rhetorical devices to *keep* your audience's attention.

Appealing to the feelings or emotions of your audience to get them on your side is an important rhetorical device.

Activity 6

1 Re-read the development of Chief Joseph's speech (repeated below) where he gives details about the misery his people have experienced. From the list below, pick out the subjects included in the second paragraph. Then place those subjects in the order in which they appear, and copy an appropriate example from the text next to each one.

> ◆ the wind   ◆ old people lost   ◆ nothing to drink   ◆ the weather
> ◆ no shelter   ◆ no blankets   ◆ missing children   ◆ nothing to eat

> It is cold, and we have no blankets. The little children are freezing to death. My people, some of them, have run away to the hills, and have no blankets, no food. No one knows where they are – perhaps freezing to death. I want to have time to look for my children, and see how many of them I can find. Maybe I shall find them among the dead.

2 Working in pairs or small groups, discuss how the details Chief Joseph includes would make his listeners feel sorry for him and his people.

Activity 7 ⓦⓢ

1 Look back at the plan you made in Activity 3, where you listed points to develop your main idea.
Use your notes to write the next section of your speech.
Develop each of your points in detail.

2 Remember your aim is get your listeners on your side. Include vocabulary that is likely to make your listeners sympathise with you. Here are some suitable words and phrases.

> ◆ worn out   ◆ exhausted   ◆ waste of time   ◆ weary

A powerful ending

Now look again at the ending of Chief Joseph's speech (repeated below). Here, words have been chosen to make sure that listeners do not forget his message.

> Hear me, my chiefs! I am tired. My heart is sick and sad. From where the sun stands I will fight no more forever.

Activity 8 ⓦ

Find examples of rhetorical devices from Chief Joseph's speech, this time from the ending. Copy and complete this chart. Write an example from the speech of each device in the second column. In the third column match the correct phrase from the list below to describe the effect on the audience.

Device	Example	Effect
Words beginning with the same sound placed next to each other for effect (alliteration)	sick and sad	d
Talks straight to the audience		
Last word emphasises overall message		
Attention is drawn to ideas by using dramatic effects such as pauses		
Words chosen to make the listener share the speaker's feelings		

Effects

a Makes audience feel sorry for speaker.

b Makes audience listen because they are being spoken to directly.

c Carries the audience along with the speaker, helping them to identify with the speaker's point of view.

d Emphasises the words.

e Leaves the audience with a very clear message.

Activity 9 ⓌⓈ

Now write the ending of your own speech. Your aim is to convince your listeners that they should agree with you and to leave them with a message they will remember. Include some of the devices you identified in Activity 8 and remember to use simple sentences. Here are some words and phrases you may find helpful.

◆ listen to me   ◆ think carefully   ◆ finally

Revising and editing your speech

Remember that you have prepared this speech to persuade others to agree with you, to get them on your side. To find out whether or not your speech is successful, read it aloud to a partner and ask him or her to assess whether it is a persuasive and convincing speech.

Here are some prompts for your partner.

> Show me how you grabbed the attention of your audience at the beginning of your speech.

> What details did you include to make your ideas clear?

> Could you add more words to make readers feel sorry for you?

> Have you used a thesaurus to find extra words?

> How many rhetorical devices have you used in your speech? Show me where.

> Have you used punctuation to emphasise your meaning? For example:
> ◆ a comma to create a pause
> ◆ a question mark to appeal directly to your listeners
> ◆ an exclamation mark to draw attention to parts of the speech you would like to have special emphasis.

> Show me where you have used short sentences to sum up your message at the end of your speech.

Make the alterations suggested by your partner, then use the prompts to help him (or her) improve his speech.

The final stage is to give your speech to your class. Before you do this, work through the activities in Unit 18, which will help you to develop your speech-making techniques.

In this unit you will learn how to:

- give advice to a particular audience
- gain the attention of your readers
- make use of different presentational devices
- use argument and counter-argument to meet the objections of your readers.

Giving advice to a particular audience

Read the text below, which is from an advice leaflet on drugs called 'The Score'. It has been written for a teenage audience.

1 **DRUGS? WHAT'S THE BIG DEAL?**

2 Everyone has something to say about drugs. Even so, it's still an issue wrapped in myths, and often fiction gets in the way of facts.

3 Knowing the score isn't just about knowing the buzz different drugs can give. It's also about being aware of the effects they can have on your mind, your body and even the way you live your life. There are serious risks linked to drug taking, so it's vital to get your hands on information you can trust …

4 'The Score' puts you squarely in the picture about drugs. It answers questions, sorts problems, explains the risks and drops in on **dilemmas** and debates.

5 Whatever your viewpoint – there's something inside for everyone.

And if it's pure info you're after, our drug files are one essential source you'll return to again and again.

*from **The Score: Facts About Drugs** by National Drugs Helpline*

Word bank
dilemmas – choices between equally unattractive options

Activity 1

1 The different sections of the text on page 135 have been numbered. To help you understand how the text has been organised, match up the items on the list below with the numbers on the text.
   a Tells readers it's important to read information they can trust.
   b Invites readers to read on in the leaflet.
   c Opening statement, everyone knows something about drugs.
   d Title with a question to appeal to readers.
   e Tells readers how the booklet can help them.

2 Think about the target audience, which is young people.
   a Why do you think the text has been organised into short paragraphs?
   b Why might it be appropriate for the writer to write in short paragraphs for this particular audience?

Activity 2

1 The title of the text on page 135 contains the sort of language you are likely to hear in conversation, but would not necessarily use in writing.
   a Write down the phrase from the title that you are more likely to say than to write.
   b Write down two more words or phrases from the text that you are more likely to use in conversation than in writing.

2 This text appeals to young people by making them feel they are being spoken to directly. The writers do this by using the pronoun 'you' and the adjective 'your'.
   a How many times throughout the text do the writers use these words?
   b Why do you think they have used them so often?

Activity 3 🔷

1 Read these sentences about smoking.

   ◆ It is very easy to get addicted to smoking.
   ◆ Many young people smoke because their friends do.
   ◆ Smoking is very expensive.
   ◆ Smokers are more likely to suffer coughs and chest problems.

   The first sentence could be changed as follows. What differences can you spot?

   > It is very easy to get addicted to smoking. ➔ It's easy for you to get hooked on smoking.

2 Rewrite the other sentences using language that will appeal to young people.

Using punctuation to draw attention to your meaning

Writers use punctuation to draw attention to their text, to make their readers take notice of what they are saying to them.

Look at the title of the text on page 135: 'Drugs? What's the Big Deal?' Why do you think the writers have used a question mark in the title? What effect does this have on the reader?

Activity 4

1 Rewrite the following titles using a question mark to appeal directly to readers. You may have to add words of your own or miss some out to turn the sentences into questions.

> ◆ Smoking is no big deal
> ◆ Some facts you need to know about smoking

2 Look at paragraph 3 of the text on page 135, where the writers end the last sentence with a row of dots.

> There are serious risks linked to drug taking, so it's vital to get your hands on information you can trust …

These dots are known as an **ellipsis**. Writers use this punctuation mark when they want to show that they have left some information out or they have not finished a sentence.

Read the sentence again and work out why the writers have used an ellipsis. What do they want readers to think or do?

3 Working in pairs, read the following sentences and decide which of them you could end with an ellipsis to make readers read on.

◆ Nicotine is a very powerful drug.
◆ Smoking can be the cause of many serious diseases, for example emphysema, lung cancer and many more.
◆ Many smokers wish they had never started smoking.

4 One reason why the text has a friendly informal tone is because it uses lots of shortened words. For example, in 'What's the big deal?' the words 'what is' have been shortened with an apostrophe (') to show where the letter 'i' has been missed out.

Find and write down five more examples of shortened words from the text on page 135. Next to them write the full version of the words.

Activity 5

Write the **first draft** of a page for an advice booklet on smoking. Aim to write three paragraphs. Use the facts in the box below as well as your own ideas. Keep your first draft as you will need it for reworking in Activity 7.

Smoking fact box

- Tobacco contains nicotine.
- This drug is very addictive.
- Its effects are very fast.
- First-time smokers can feel sick.
- Ten cigarettes a day cost £500 per year or more.
- Breathing in other people's smoke can cause breathing difficulties, asthma, cancer.
- Smoking can make your breath, hair and clothes smell.
- It's illegal for shopkeepers to sell tobacco to under 16s.
- The largest single group of new smokers is teenage girls.

Before you begin, think about your purpose: this is to **advise** young people against smoking. The style of writing you will use is conversational, as you must sound as if you are talking to your readers.

Step 1: Begin by putting the following headings in the order you will use them in your writing.

- Health issues
- Reasons why people like to smoke
- Expense
- The effect on other people

Select facts from the fact box to go under each. Number the facts in the order you will use them.

Step 2: Choose a title that will get your readers interested straightaway.

Step 3: Write your first paragraph. Think carefully about your topic sentence (the first sentence), which introduces the subject of smoking to your readers. Use your first set of facts to write the first section of your advice.

Step 4: Now write your second and third paragraphs. Begin each one with a topic sentence to introduce what you will write about in that paragraph.

Step 5: When you have completed your draft, work with a partner and ask him/her to underline places where you have used:

- language you would hear in conversation
- the shortened form of words
- punctuation to get the attention of your readers.

Matching presentation and structure to audience and purpose

Another way of making sure your text gets the attention of your readers is to use **presentational devices**. A presentational device is something that makes your text look different on the page. Writers use colour, different sizes and fonts, headings and sub-headings to catch the attention of their readers. Sometimes they use pictures as well.

Look closely at the text below. Do you recognise it? It is exactly the same as the one on page 135, but here it *looks* very different and is more likely to gain the attention of readers because of the way it is presented. Work with a partner to list the differences between this text and the one on page 135.

DRUGS? WHAT'S THE BIG DEAL...?

EVERYONE has something to say about drugs. Even so, it's still an issue wrapped in *Myths*, and often **fiction** gets in the way of the FACTS.

Knowing the SCORE isn't just about knowing the buzz different drugs can give. It's also about being aware of the effects they can have on your mind, your body and even the way you live your life. There are S E R I O U S risks linked to drug taking, so it's **VITAL** to get your hands on information you can TRUST...

The SCORE puts you squarely in the picture about drugs. It answers QUESTIONS, sorts PROBLEMS, explains the RISKS and drops in on *dilemmas* and DEBATES. Whatever your viewpoint — there's something inside for everyone.

And if it's **pure info** you're after, our DRUG FILES are one essential source you'll return to again and again.

*From **The Score: Facts about Drugs** by National Drugs Helpline*

Activity 6

Read through the items in the columns below. Presentational devices and effects have been placed in the wrong order. Match up the presentational devices with the correct effects. Look at the colour version of 'The Score' (page 139) to help you.

Presentational devices	Effects
1 **Large bold type**	a Makes text interesting for readers to read
2 Coloured background	b Emphasises individual words
3 Underlining	c Draws attention to key points
4 Use of colour for individual words	d Draws attention to whole text
5 Different size letters	e Makes text look interesting at first sight
6 *Different* fonts	f Makes title stand out

Activity 7

Look again at the draft text you wrote on smoking in Activity 5. Rewrite this text using the presentational devices you have just identified. Use the text on page 139 to help you. Follow Steps 1 to 3 below and read the prompts.

Step 1: Rewrite your draft text. Check that you have:

- ◆ put your advice across in a friendly way
- ◆ used language that is used by young people in conversation.

Step 2: Make notes on the text to show where you will use different presentational devices. Think about how to:

make your text look interesting enough to attract readers' attention

make your headings stand out clearly and attract attention to key points

use different sizes and styles of fonts to draw attention to key words

use background colour to draw attention to your text

emphasise your headings

add pictures to make your text look even more interesting

Use this example to help you.

My title, use large type, bold letters red print.

Background colour pale yellow.

> Are you hooked on smoking?
> *Do you find you are short of money* at the end of the week? This could be because you are spending too much money on cigarettes. Surely you have worked it out by now? **Smoking is expensive!**

Different font, larger letters.

Underline 'too much money'.

Different colour, blue, larger type, different font.

Step 3: Write your final draft building in all of your presentational devices.

Using argument and counter-argument

Giving advice can be difficult. Sometimes the person you are advising has an answer for everything you tell them. If you want to persuade them to take your advice, you need to have answers ready for their objections. You need to work out in advance what objections they might make.

You will remember that arguing against a point somebody makes is known as using **counter-argument**.

The following example is taken from a discussion between two students about alcohol.

Argument. — [*You say you have more fun when you drink alcohol,*] [*but*] [*remember you can still have a good party without alcohol. It's the people who come to your party that make it fun.*]

Counter-argument. —

Comma and word 'but' separate the two sides of the argument.

Activity 8

Match up the following statements about alcohol (listed 1–3) with the correct counter-argument (listed a–c). Remember to use a comma and the word 'but' at the beginning of the counter-argument.

Statements

1 You say everyone does silly things when they are drunk ...
2 Some people say drinking is part of growing up ...
3 You think getting drunk every now and then does no one any harm ...

Counter-arguments

a ... it's illegal to buy alcohol under the age of 18.
b ... 1,000 children under the age of 15 are admitted to hospital each year with acute alcohol poisoning.
c ... alcohol affects your judgement making you do things you regret later.

Using counter-argument to give advice

Read the letter on page 142. It was written by a young person who needs some advice. As you read, make a note of the problems of each side of the argument under these headings:

Parents	Teenager

Dear Paul,

I need some advice about dealing with my parents.

Everyone else in my class goes to parties and drinks and has a good time. My parents won't let me go to parties because they say everyone will be drinking and I'm not allowed to. They say there's always trouble at parties where people drink and they don't want me breaking the law by drinking under the age of 18.

I'm missing out on a lot of fun because my parents are mean and old-fashioned.

What can I do?

A bored and lonely teenager.

Activity 9 WS

Write the reply from Paul giving advice to Bored and Lonely.

1 This is what you will have to do:

- ◆ show Bored and Lonely that you sympathise with him
- ◆ help him to realise that his parents might have a point
- ◆ help him to understand that perhaps he is too young to drink alcohol
- ◆ expect that he might not be very pleased with your advice
- ◆ present your ideas in way that he will accept, perhaps by offering other choices for him to make.

2 Use these sentence starters to help you:

> You have got problems with your parents but …
> Think about your parents and …
> Things are difficult …
> Maybe you could …
> It might be possible for you …

Presenting advice in an impersonal way

So far you have given advice to a particular person or a group of people. You have addressed your readers directly using the pronoun 'you' and the sort of language that your readers can relate to. You have used a **personal** style. For example, you will remember this sentence from 'The Score':

> … our drug files are one essential resource you'll return to again and again.

The use of the pronoun 'you' in this sentence makes readers feel they are being addressed personally.

Sometimes advice is presented in an **impersonal** way. This means that it is not addressed directly to a particular group of readers. Look at the same sentence written in an impersonal way.

> The drug files are essential resources that can be returned to again and again.

Can you spot the differences between this sentence and the first one? What words have been taken away to make the second sentence impersonal?

When you are reading impersonal advice you sometimes have to work out what the writer is advising you to do because it is not explained to you directly.

Activity 10

Read this text in which advice is presented in an impersonal way.

> Alcohol is a depressant drug. It slows down the nervous system, reactions and the way the body functions.
> **A** *Drinking too much can lead to lack of consciousness.*
> Users then risk choking on their own vomit.
> **B** *This can kill.*

Sentence **A** could contain this 'hidden' advice:
don't drink too much or this could happen to you.

1   Work with a partner to work out the 'hidden' advice in sentence **B**. Copy out sentence **B**, then write your 'hidden' advice next to it.

2   Now read the rest of the text below and work out the 'hidden' advice for each of the sentences with letters.

> **C** *A thousand children are admitted to hospital each year with alcoholic poisoning.*
> Around half of all pedestrians aged 16 to 60 killed in road accidents have more alcohol in their blood stream than the legal drink–drive limit.
> Alcohol can affect how people feel, what they do and why they do things.
> **D** *Alcohol is something to treat with respect and to be in control of.*
> **E** *Making decisions and learning to be in control is part of becoming an adult.*

Activity 11 ICT WS

Look at this piece of writing, which offers direct advice in a personal way. Your task is to change it from a personal to an impersonal style. Your audience will be anyone who needs advice on this subject – not any specific group.

I am sure you know solvents are found in everyday items such as glue, lighter fuel, hairspray, some paints and correcting fluids. It can be very dangerous for you to sniff solvents. Did you know that sniffing gases, glues or aerosols kills one person every week?

Some young people like to sniff glue or aerosols because doing this makes them feel giggly and dreamy. When you are under the influence of solvents you can have accidents because you do not really understand what you are doing. Sometimes you can have hallucinations (see or hear things that are not really there). This can be a very frightening experience if this happens to you.

You run a lot of risks if you sniff glue or solvents. You can damage your lungs or your heart or even suffocate. Make sure you think about these risks before you try solvent sniffing.

Follow these steps to help you organise your work.

Step 1: Read through the text making a note of all the places where the writer uses the pronoun 'you' to create a personal tone. These are the parts of the text you will have to change to rewrite the text using an impersonal tone.

Step 2: Write your first redraft so that it has an impersonal tone. Here are some ideas.

◆ In some sentences you can miss out words to make the sentence sound more impersonal, although you might have to put in new ones. For example, 'You run a lot of risks' could be changed to 'There are a lot of risks'.

◆ Change the order of words in the sentences to make them sound impersonal. For instance, 'Make sure you think about these risks' could be changed to 'These risks should be thought about'.

◆ Use some of these impersonal sentence starters. `

> ◆ There is/There are …   ◆ It is well known that …   ◆ Solvents are …
> ◆ It can be dangerous to …   ◆ There are serious consequences …

Step 3: Read your draft aloud to a partner. Ask their advice about alterations.

Step 4: Make your alterations, then produce the final draft.

This unit will help you to:

◆ present ideas in a logical way
◆ think about different ways of organising and linking paragraphs
◆ use quotations and evidence from texts
◆ make judgements about texts
◆ write a formal essay in a set time.

Presenting ideas in a logical way

The term 'logical' means thinking things through in a clear, orderly way. When you write to analyse, you write about your examination of something. A logical analysis would be an examination based on careful reasoning, presented in a clear, easy to follow way. This could be a text, an object, a series of events or a set of ideas.

You write to analyse in a range of school subjects. For example, in History you are often asked to explain why events happen and what was the result of them.

Look at this History question:

> *Why did the plague spread so quickly across Europe and how did it change life for people there?*

The following steps show you how one student tackled this analysis.

Step 1: Read the question carefully and work out what you are expected to do. This is what the student wrote:

> What question expects me to do
> Part 1: how/why did plague spread?   Part 2: what were the effects?

Step 2: Make notes.

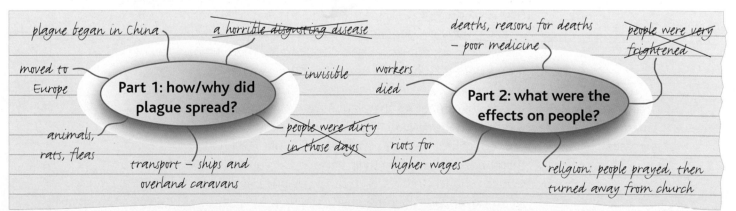

plague began in China   a horrible disgusting disease   deaths, reasons for deaths – poor medicine   people were very frightened

moved to Europe   invisible   workers died

Part 1: how/why did plague spread?   **Part 2: what were the effects on people?**

animals, rats, fleas   people were dirty in those days   riots for higher wages

transport – ships and overland caravans   religion: people prayed, then turned away from church

Why do you think the student crossed out three of the points on his original plan? Are these points directly relevant to the question?

Step 3: Make a paragraph plan.

Getting your ideas organised is a very important part of writing to analyse because you need to get the facts and events in order before you analyse the results and effects. Here is what the student wrote:

Paragraph 1
Sentence 1: topic sentence to introduce subject of plague
Sentence 2: where it started
Sentence 3: how disease was carried (animals)
Sentence 4: how disease moved into other countries

How do you think this plan will help the student to write a clear analysis?
What do you think the student has done well here?

Step 4: Write your analysis.

This is the analysis the student wrote following his plan. His thoughts on how he wrote the analysis have been placed around the text.

I have used the past tense to write about events which have taken place.

The plague came to Europe from China in the 1330s.
At this time China was one of the world's largest trading nations and therefore had many links with countries in Europe. The disease was carried by fleas and rats on ships and overland trading caravans travelling to Europe. The rats and fleas passed unnoticed into houses. They breed very quickly and so the disease spread very rapidly. In this way the disease spread very quickly throughout Europe.

My topic sentence introduces the subject of this paragraph.
I am beginning to draw conclusions.

My first paragraph gives an overall picture of events.

My topic sentence introduces the subject of this paragraph.

The plague had long-lasting effects on life in Europe. At that time doctors and the medicines they used could not deal with this deadly disease and as a result many people died from it. After five years 25 million people were dead, one-third of all the people in Europe.

The plague caused a serious shortage of workers because so many people had died from it. There were many riots as workers demanded higher wages and were refused.

I have used this phrase to link my ideas.

[Another effect] of the plague was the way people thought about religion. People had prayed to be spared from the plague and when this did not happen they began to question their belief in God and the Church. So it can be seen that the plague changed life in Europe in several ways.

My final sentence draws a conclusion; I have referred back to the title here.

Activity 1

You will have noticed that some of the words in the text opposite have been written in a different colour. These are **connectives**, words or phrases that 'glue' the text together and link the ideas. You will see that connectives can be used in several positions in a sentence or a paragraph.

Make a list of the connectives in the text so that you can use them in your own writing. Copy the chart below and sort the connectives under the appropriate headings in columns 1 and 2. An example has been done for you.

Temporal connectives (words or phrases that are to do with time)	Causal connectives (words or phrases that explain causes and effects)	Position in sentence or paragraphs
	therefore	middle of sentence

Activity 2

Look closely at the pictures and text on pages 148 and 149. They give you lots of information about the Fire of London. You are going to use this information to write about one page on the following task:

> *Analyse the reasons why the Fire of London spread so quickly and why it caused so much damage.*

Step 1: Read the question carefully and work out exactly what you are expected to do. Finish this sentence: I will have to explain …

Step 2: Make notes. Use some of the following headings to help you group your notes together. Not all of the headings are suitable for helping you to answer the question, so choose the ones most closely linked to the question.

◆ Buildings   ◆ Streets   ◆ Weather conditions
◆ People   ◆ Animals   ◆ Equipment

When you make your notes remember to:

◆ ignore any information that does not tell you *directly* about the fire and the damage (for example, you do not need to include the names of all the streets on the picture)

◆ write short phrases only because notes are a quick way of recording your ideas; full sentences are *not* necessary for notes.

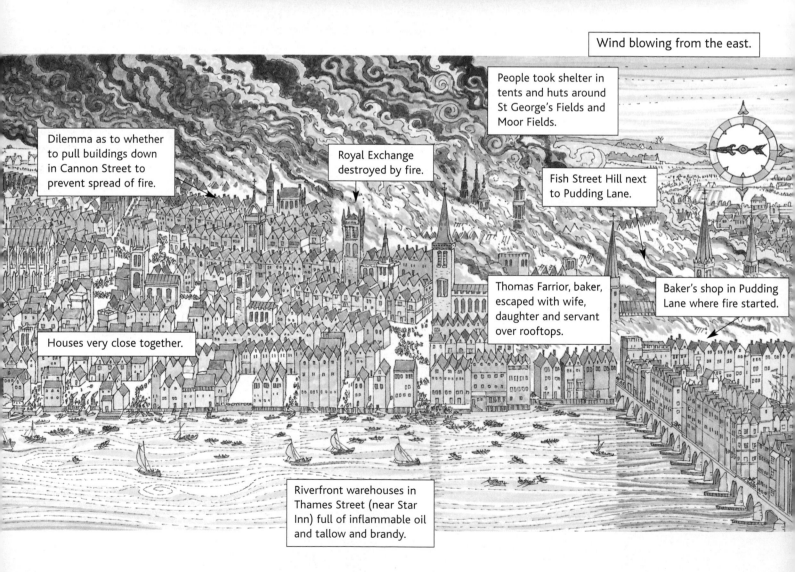

Wind blowing from the east.

People took shelter in tents and huts around St George's Fields and Moor Fields.

Dilemma as to whether to pull buildings down in Cannon Street to prevent spread of fire.

Royal Exchange destroyed by fire.

Fish Street Hill next to Pudding Lane.

Thomas Farrior, baker, escaped with wife, daughter and servant over rooftops.

Baker's shop in Pudding Lane where fire started.

Houses very close together.

Riverfront warehouses in Thames Street (near Star Inn) full of inflammable oil and tallow and brandy.

Information box

◆ 80 per cent of City of London destroyed
◆ 13,200 houses destroyed
◆ 90 parish churches
◆ Started 1 o'clock in the morning
◆ Began 2 September 1666
◆ Burned for five days
◆ Light from the fire could be seen 40 miles away
◆ Clouds of smoke stretched for nearly 50 miles

Activity 3 ICT WS

Use the notes you made in Activity 2 to write your analysis. Aim to write between eight and twelve lines in two paragraphs. Follow these steps.

Step 1: Number your notes in the order you are going to use them. Think about the order in which events happened.

Step 2: Write your opening paragraph. Introduce the topic of the Fire of London.

Step 3: Begin your account of how the fire spread. Follow the notes you have made. Remember to examine the reasons *why* the fire spread.

Step 4: Follow the order of your notes to continue your analysis.

Step 5: This is your conclusion where you sum up the damage caused by the fire. Use the information box on page 149 to help you.

Step 6: Edit and revise your analysis. Check your work by asking yourself these questions:

- Have I begun my paragraph with a topic sentence?
- Have I written about events in an order which my readers will find easy to follow?
- Have I **analysed** and **explained** the damage caused by the fire?

When you have made improvements to your work, make a final copy.

Key words and phrases
◆ destroy ◆ damage ◆ immense ◆ inflammable (burns easily)

Useful connectives
◆ because ◆ as a result of ◆ in this way ◆ therefore ◆ so

Using quotations and evidence

When you write to analyse you need to refer to a text in detail. If you copy out the exact words a writer has used, this is known as using a **quotation**. Quotations are always written in inverted commas to show that you are using someone else's words. Quoting from Samuel Pepys's diary, you could write:

> When describing the damage caused by the Fire of London, Samuel Pepys referred to 'the cracking of houses at their ruin'.

Now read some more of Samuel Pepys's writing about the Fire of London.

2 September 1666

You were almost burned with a shower of firedrops. We saw the fire as only one entire arch of fire from this to the other side of the bridge. It made me weep to see it. The churches, houses, and all on fire
5 and flaming at once, and a horrid noise the flames made, and the cracking of houses at their ruine.

 We were forced to pack up our own goods and prepare for their removal.

*Adapted from **Samuel Pepys's Diary***

Look at the extract below from a student's analysis of this extract. The student had been asked to analyse the ways in which Pepys made the fire seem real.

> When Samuel Pepys says 'you were almost burned with a shower of firedrops', this **suggests** that there were so many sparks in the sky that walking underneath them was like being rained upon.

The quotation is followed by a comment on the meaning of Samuel Pepys's words. The comment **analyses** and **explains** the quotation. It does not repeat the words of the quotation. The comment is introduced by the phrase 'this suggests'. Other useful phrases for introducing your analysis of quotations are:

◆ this shows …   ◆ this tells the reader that …
◆ this makes me think …   ◆ this implies …

Remember: quotation + comment = analysis

Activity 4

For each of the following sentences find the right quotation from Samuel Pepys's diary, then make your comment.

1 Pepys helps readers to understand that the fire burned across the whole river when he says ……………… . The word 'arch' tells the reader that ……………… .

2 Samuel Pepys was very upset by the fire. He writes ……………………. . This shows ……………… .

3 Life was not easy during the Fire of London. You can tell this because Pepys writes ……………… . This makes me think ……………… .

Making judgements about texts

When you write to analyse a text you sometimes make judgements about it. This is different from a expressing your personal opinion, such as 'I don't like this' or 'This poem doesn't interest me'. A judgement is always based on evidence from the text.

Read the poem 'Thunder and Lightning', where the poet builds up a clear picture of a powerful storm. Students were asked to analyse how the poet does this.

Thunder and Lightning

Blood punches through every vein
As lightning **strips** the windowpane.

Under its flashing whip, a white
Village leaps to light.

5 On tubs of thunder, fists of rain
Slog it out of sight again.

Blood **punches** the heart with fright
As rain **belts** the village night.

James Kirkup

One student began his analysis with this comment:

Judgement. ─────── [I think the poem has a dramatic beginning] [because the poet
Evidence. ─────── has chosen the word 'punches', which sounds powerful.]

Activity 5

Complete sentences 1–4 under 'Judgements' with one of the phrases a–d under 'Evidence'. Work with a partner to match up the correct evidence from the poem above to support each judgement. Then write out each complete sentence.

Judgements
1 This is a good technique to use because the poet makes the thunder seem as if it is a <u>person</u> attacking the village when he writes …
2 It is easy for the reader to understand the power of the storm …
3 I think the writer uses an effective way to say that the storm moved quickly …
4 The villagers' fear is emphasised well in the line …

Evidence
a 'blood punches the heart with fright'.   b in the line 'under its flashing whip'.
c the line 'fists of rain'.   d violent vocabulary such as 'slog' and 'belts'.

Analysing a poem in exam conditions

Often in exams you are asked to analyse a poem. These are the steps you should follow.

Steps for analysis	Example
1 Read the question carefully.	
2 Underline key words in the question – the ones that tell you exactly what to do.	How well does the poet build up a clear picture of the power of the storm in the poem 'Thunder and Lightning'?

'How well' means make my own judgements

'power' tells me to look for words that show the strength of the storm

'build up' means start from the beginning and work through the poem

3 Read through the poem carefully, thinking about what the question has asked you to look for.	
4 Read the poem again, this time underlining the quotations you will use as evidence.	Blood punches through every vein As lightning strips the windowpane.
5 Write the first paragraph of your answer; refer to the question in your first sentence.	The poet is very successful in building up a picture of a powerful storm.
6 Work through your evidence bit by bit. Don't forget to use evidence (quotations) to support your judgements.	The poet writes 'lightning strips the windowpane. / Under its flashing whip'. The idea of a whip is effective because it helps the reader understand that the lightning appeared very quickly, like the crack of a whip.
7 At the end of your analysis refer back to the question to make your final judgement.	The last two lines of the poem sum up the power of the storm. The poet refers to the 'fright' the storm causes and also uses a powerful word, 'belts', to show the strength of the storm. The word 'night' suggests a dark and dramatic setting for the storm. Throughout the poem the poet has convinced readers that the storm is powerful and frightening.

Activity 6 ICT WS

Now try analysing a poem for yourself. This is the question you are going to answer:

How well do you think the poet has created a mysterious atmosphere for the opening of 'The Listeners'?

Step 1: Read the beginning of 'The Listeners' below carefully. The poem has been annotated to help you understand the techniques the poet uses to builds up an atmosphere of mystery and tension.

Poem begins with question.

The Listeners

'Is there anybody there?' said the Traveller,

Knocking on the moonlit door;

And his horse in the silence **champed** the grasses

Of the forest's ferny floor:

And a bird flew up out of the **turret**,

Above the Traveller's head:

And he **smote** upon the door again a second time;

'Is there anybody there?' he said.

But no one descended to the Traveller;

No head from the leaf-fringed sill

Leaned over and looked into his grey eyes,

Where he stood **perplexed** and still. …

from **The Listeners** *by Walter De La Mare*

Poem is set at night time.

Alliteration of letter 'f' creates soft, gentle sounds.

Question repeated, makes reader wonder what is going on.

The word 'no' repeated to stress that he is alone.

Word bank

champed – chewed
turret – small tower on a house
smote – banged hard
perplexed – puzzled

Step 2: Follow Steps 1 to 7 on page 153 to help you plan your answer. Use the plan below to help you structure your analysis.

Paragraph 1	Opening statement based on the title: I think the poet … Take the first two techniques annotated on page 154 and say whether or not you think they are effective in building up a sense of mystery.
Paragraph 2	Take the next three techniques and make judgements about them in the same way.
Paragraph 3	Write a final statement in which you sum up your judgement about the poem.

Key words and phrases
◆ effective ◆ good ◆ very well ◆ atmosphere ◆ helps to create

Useful connectives
◆ because ◆ as a result of ◆ in this way ◆ therefore

Remember to:

◆ give short examples from the poem
◆ put inverted commas round your quotations
◆ support your opinions and judgements with evidence from the poem.

Aim to spend about half an hour on this task.

Part 1
Writing to inform

Write an information leaflet on the Blue Cross, an animal charity, telling readers about the work that the charity does with animals. Read the notes below, then follow Steps 1 to 4 opposite to help you organise your writing. You should write three or four paragraphs. Address your readers directly to make the information seem more personal.

BLUE CROSS STARTED IN 1897
Believes in helping all animals
Believes no animal in need should be turned away

- Large and well-known charity
- Takes in homeless, unwanted animals
- Provides new homes for animals
- In recent years there has been an increase in number of animals needing help
- A large charity: runs four animal hospitals and clinics
- 11 animal rescue centres
- Free treatment provided for sick and injured animals
- Last year took in over 8,000 cats, dogs, horses

- Only source of money: donations from public
- No government funding (money) for the organisation
- Very expensive caring for animals
- Romany: 10 weeks old, abandoned kitten, given a home
- Jodie: starving puppy, rescued and fed
- Zebedee: neglected horse, rescued and restored to health

THE BLUE CROSS
Animal Welfare Charity

Step 1:

Begin by sorting the notes. Write the following headings in your exercise book. As you read through the list, put each note under an appropriate heading. If you wish, you could choose your own headings.

- ◆ General information about the Blue Cross: background, beliefs, size and importance
- ◆ What the Blue Cross actually does to help animals
- ◆ How much it costs to run the charity and where the money comes from

Step 2:

Organise your ideas into three paragraphs. Look at your notes and decide which order you will put them in when you write your full sentences. Put a number next to the points in the order in which you will use them.

Writing reminders

- ◆ Begin with general statement to introduce topic to your readers.
- ◆ Use the present tense to describe the work the organisation does now.
- ◆ Link your information with connectives such as: also, in addition, another, as well as, furthermore.
- ◆ Think about the ways you could present the information to make it clear for readers.
- ◆ How could you use headings and different fonts to make the information stand out?

Step 3:

Read through your work and ask yourself these questions.

- ◆ Have I given enough information to my readers?
- ◆ Will they understand the work the Blue Cross does after reading my information leaflet?
- ◆ Have I linked my ideas clearly using at least three different connectives?
- ◆ Have I missed out any words anywhere?
- ◆ How will my leaflet look to readers? What could I do to improve on the presentation? For example, do I need to include more headings? Do I need to use different sizes of type to emphasise key points?

Step 4:

Make any alterations you think necessary, then write your final draft.

Part 2
Writing to explain

Many young people feel strongly about how some animals are treated. Choose a topic you feel strongly about and explain in detail why you feel this way. Follow Steps 1 to 5 below to help you organise your writing.

Step 1:

Choose your topic, for example: cruelty to animals, bullying in schools, lack of facilities for young people in the area where you live.

Step 2:

◆ Make a list of the reasons why you feel strongly about your chosen topic.

◆ Number your reasons in the order in which you intend to write about them.

◆ Will you use your strongest reason first or save it to the end?

Step 3:

Make a paragraph plan for your writing like this one.

Opening paragraph	Introduce my topic to my readers, what I feel strongly about
Paragraph 2	My first set of reasons for feeling strongly about this
Paragraph 3	My next set of reasons
Paragraph 4	My conclusion, sum up my feelings

Writing reminders

◆ Write mainly in the present tense.

◆ Use causal connectives to explain your feelings, for example:
  because, as a result of this, for this reason, in this way, so.

◆ Include evidence such as things you have heard or seen to support your explanations.

Step 4:

Read through your work, check that your explanations and reasons come across clearly to your readers.

Step 5:

Make any changes you think are necessary. Write your final draft.

Section E ◆ Speaking and listening ⬩CT⬩
Introduction

It's very easy to take speaking and listening for granted because they are things you do every day almost without thinking about them. But there are skills you can learn and develop.

Over the last two years of Key Stage 3 you will have been given the opportunity to speak and listen in a wide range of different contexts. You will have made presentations on your own. You will have worked in groups of different sizes and you will have used drama to explore ideas. The units in this section extend that range of contexts even further and present a wider range of skills to develop and situations to work in.

In Unit 18, *Making presentations*, you will explore how speech-makers use language in special ways to have an effect on their audience. You will learn how to develop your own ideas in spoken language.

In Unit 19, *Drama in speaking and listening*, you will look at how ideas have been explored in drama by playwrights before developing your own approach to an issue using dramatic techniques.

In Unit 20, *Working together*, you will focus on listening skills and working together on ideas using interview techniques.

Unit 21 tests you on the skills you will develop as you work carefully through the three units.

18 Making presentations

This unit will help you to:
- ◆ consider your abilities as a speaker in a range of situations
- ◆ use standard English to explain ideas
- ◆ identify the underlying themes of a talk.

Thinking about speaking

We speak in a range of situations. Most are informal, fairly ordinary situations such as chatting with friends or asking for goods in a shop. But there are also some more formal, less frequent kinds of situation such as having to talk to a classroom full of people.

Activity 1 ⬥ WS

1 Working on your own, use a chart like the one below to make some notes about your abilities as a speaker in different situations. In each case try to think of an explanation for your answer (there are some prompts in the third column).

Question	Think ...	My notes
With what kinds of people am I most and least confident in conversation?	You might think about how you feel with family, friends, older people, strangers, members of the opposite sex, etc.	Why?
In what kinds of situations am I most and least confident?	You might think about informal situations like chatting, being on the phone or face to face; and more formal situations like speaking in front of the class. What about being in a small group in class?	I'm confident when ... I'm less confident when ... Why?
Do I talk to my parents in a different style from the way I talk to my friends?	Think about the kinds of words you use; do you shorten words? Do you speak to your parents in a different tone?	Why?
Do I talk with friends differently in a small-group classroom discussion from the way I talk with them outside school?	Think about how much you contribute, how freely you speak, and whether there are different 'rules' for when and how you speak.	Why?
Does my style of speech change when I stand at the front of the class to speak?	Think about your use of language. Do you speak more slowly? Loudly?	Why?

2 When you have completed the chart, discuss your responses in small groups of four or five. Talk about each question, and what similarities and differences you can see in your responses.

3 Now make a few written notes about the following.
   a Your **strengths** as a speaker. For example, you might write:
   'I think my speaking is very good when I'm chatting with friends and family about things I know about.'
   b What you would like to **target for improvement**. For example, you might write: 'I'd like to be more confident in more situations. I think I can achieve that by trying to contribute more in small groups to begin with.'

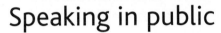

Speaking in public

You have spent some time reflecting on your own abilities as a speaker. Activity 2 will involve you in preparing a very short piece of public speaking.

First, here is the text of a brief talk about something that irritates the speaker. Next to it are some notes about it. Read the talk – in the left-hand column – on its own. Then read it again looking at the notes on the right.

The Talk	Notes
If there is one thing that really irritates me it is queues at the checkouts in supermarkets.	The talk is very brief, only 45 seconds, so it is a good idea to introduce the subject quickly.
There's a law. Whichever queue you choose to stand in, something will go wrong: the till roll runs out; the shopper at the front has an argument about the price of potatoes; someone's credit card doesn't work and his/her other card is buried at the bottom of a bag; the checkout assistant turns out to be a trainee who doesn't know a banana from a baked bean; there's a horrible little toddler who insists on putting every item of shopping on to the conveyor belt himself. Very, very slowly. Meanwhile, the queue you decided not to join because it looked longer is zipping the shoppers through at the speed of light.	This is the main body of the talk. In this section there is a kind of list of details about **what** irritates the speaker. To help make the point, the speaker uses some contrast: 'very slowly' / 'the speed of light'
The more in a rush you are, the longer you have to wait in the queue. You can't win.	This is the conclusion of the talk. There is a snappy final statement, which acts like a full stop to show the audience the talk has ended.

This talk has a beginning, a middle and an end. Working in pairs, discuss the following statements and decide for each one whether you: agree/disagree/are not sure.

1 A good beginning should let the audience know what the talk is about.
2 The middle section of a talk should be the longest.
3 A good conclusion should repeat the main point of the talk.

Activity 2 ⓦⓢ

You are to give a 45-second talk to your class about something that really irritates or annoys you. You will not have to use very formal language: you know your audience and they know you.

Use the following steps to help you plan your 45-second talk.

Step 1: Decide on a topic, a pet hate. Here are some ideas.

◆ Homework
◆ A particular kind of television programme
◆ Something fashionable
◆ Someone famous
◆ Certain kinds of behaviour: spitting, swearing, showing off

Brainstorm a few ideas. Choose one.

Step 2: The next stage is to think about the different sections.

◆ **A beginning.** Let the audience know what you're going to talk about. You could start in a very straightforward way: 'Something that really irritates me is …'.

◆ **A middle section.** This is the main body of the talk. Give details about the thing that irritates you and a couple of reasons why.

◆ **A conclusion.** You want something snappy that will give a sign that you have finished. A short sentence. Think about the title or name of the pet hate – that might give you an idea: '*Home and Away* – I wish *it* would go away!'

Step 3: Write out a script for your speech so that you can time it.

Step 4: Deliver your speech. Nearly all speech makers have the full script of their speech in front of them but it is important to have eye contact with your audience. You need to decide whether you will learn your script or you may decide to use prompt cards – for 45 seconds you will only need three or four prompts. With prompts like the ones on page 163 you might have to glance down only four or five times.

You can pause between prompts to help you slow down. It might also be possible to use illustrations as prompts – little drawings that remind you of the point you want to make.

Example of a prompt card

> – One thing – checkout queues
> – There's a law – till roll / argument
>   / credit card / trainee / toddler
> – Meanwhile ...
> – More rush longer wait. Can't win

Step 5: When you have delivered your talk and listened to other students in the class making theirs, make a few notes on the following questions.

1 How good was the content of your talk? Was it interesting for the audience?

2 How well did you express yourself?

3 What are the benefits of planning?

Looking at language and structure

In making your own quite short speech to the class you probably used the kind of language you ordinarily use with your friends. On more formal occasions speeches need to be made in standard English. The main reason is that such speeches are often intended to be heard by a large audience so it is important to use a form of language easily understood by all. Can you think of other reasons why people like politicians usually speak in standard English?

To make the 'message' clear for listeners, speeches often:

◆ are clearly broken down into separate stages
◆ contain 'memorable' phrases
◆ use repetition to emphasise points.

In Activities 3 to 6 you are going to explore ways in which speeches might include these techniques.

Activity 3 (ws)

The speech on page 164 was made in 1994 by a man called Nelson Mandela. In 1990 he was released from prison. He had been imprisoned for 27 years because he fought against racial prejudice in South Africa. In 1994 he was elected as President in the country's first free elections. What follows is part of the speech he made at the ceremony when he became President. He spoke about his country.

Step 1: First, keep your book closed while your teacher reads the speech to you. As you listen, make notes on the following:

◆ 'memorable' phrases ◆ repetition to emphasise points.

Step 2: Then, working in small groups of four or five, share the notes and see if any special phrases stand out to more than one of you? Discuss between yourselves why you think these phrases stand out. Then share them with the rest of the class, giving your thoughts as to why they seem special.

Freedom from oppression

W
p.200

We dedicate this day to all the heroes and heroines in this country and the rest of the world who sacrificed in many ways and surrendered their lives so that we could be free. Their dreams have become reality. Freedom is their reward.

We are both humbled and **elevated** by the honour and privilege that you, the people
5 of South Africa, have bestowed on us, as the first President of a united, democratic, non-racial and non-sexist South Africa, to lead our country out of the valley of darkness.

We understand it still that there is no easy road to freedom. We know it well that none of us acting alone can achieve success. We must therefore act together as a united people, for national **reconciliation**, for nation building, for the birth of a new world. Let
10 there be justice for all. Let there be peace for all. Let there be work, bread, water and salt for all.

Let each know that for each the body, the mind and the soul have been freed to fulfil themselves.

Never, never and never again shall it be that this beautiful land will
15 again experience the **oppression** of one by another and suffer the indignity of being the **skunk** of the world.

Let freedom reign. The sun shall never set on so glorious a human achievement. God bless Africa. Thank you.

Nelson Mandela

Word bank
elevated – lifted up
reconciliation – settling of differences
oppression – unjust treatment
skunk – most unrespected (from the animal that smells dreadful)

Activity 4

Now look at the text of Mandela's speech. Work in small groups of four or five.

| Step 1: | **The structure**

This part of the speech is in six quite short paragraphs. Copy and complete the table below. Some examples have been done for you.

Key points of each paragraph	Key words/phrases
1 PAST sacrifices	'who sacrificed'
2 People of TODAY have honoured him	
3 Working towards the FUTURE	
4 Opportunities for EVERYONE	'for each … freed to fulfil themselves'
5 The PAST will never happen again	
6 CONCLUDES	

| Step 2: | **Repetition**

a The speaker uses quite a lot of repetition of words and phrases, e.g. he repeatedly begins sentences with 'We …'. What is the importance of that word?

b Another example of repetition is 'Never, never and never again'. Why do you think he decided to say the word three times instead of once or twice?

You made a 45-second informal speech in Activity 2 and you have now explored a quite famous historical speech. In the next activity you are going to try a more formal speech of your own.

Activity 5

Now deliver a speech of about 30 seconds using some of the skills you have been exploring:

◆ using a formal style, avoiding shortened words and slang – unless for a particular reason
◆ trying to find some 'memorable' phrases
◆ using repetition to emphasise points
◆ having a clear structure.

Choose someone to whom you could pay a tribute. That means speaking about the person's good qualities and praising them. You could praise your parents or a friend, or a famous person you know a little about.

Step 1: Choose your subject.

Step 2: Brainstorm some ideas of the qualities you wish to describe and praise. For example, if you choose your parents or a friend as a subject, think about:

- sacrifices they have made for you
- their willingness to help you
- their patience
- how they've been there for you in times of trouble.

This isn't the kind of talk in which you will tell stories about the person. If your friend once saved you from what could have been a violent situation you are not going to tell the story of what happened; you are simply going to highlight the quality your friend showed, which might be bravery.

Step 3: Organise your ideas. As you did in Activity 2, break your talk down into:

- **a beginning:** to get the attention of your audience
- **a middle section:** in which you deliver the praise
- **a conclusion:** let your audience know the talk has ended and leave them with something memorable.

Jot down some ideas for each separate section. Remember the speech is to be very brief: there is only time to highlight two or three qualities.

Step 4: Write a first draft. Read it through and check that:

- there is no slang or shortening of words
- there is some evidence of repetition. For example, you might use something like: *I thank you for … for … and for …* or *You were there for me when … and when …*
- you've tried to use one or two striking phrases rather than just using more 'obvious' words.

Step 5: Show your final draft to a partner and ask him (or her) for his opinion as to whether your talk includes the right kinds of uses of language. Make any changes you feel are necessary before you deliver your speech in front of the class. (Look back at Step 4 in Activity 2 for tips on delivering your speech.)

Step 6: When you have delivered your speech and listened to others, write down your responses to the following.

- Was my speech successful?
- Did I use some of the techniques I explored in previous activities?
- What could be improved?

One of the most famous speeches of the twentieth century was made by an American called Martin Luther King. It is known as the 'I have a dream speech' because he used that phrase several times as he spoke. You could find the speech on the Internet or in some books about the United States in the 1960s.

Martin Luther King's dream was for America to be a land in which people of all colours would live in harmony but, of course, different people have different dreams.

Activity 6

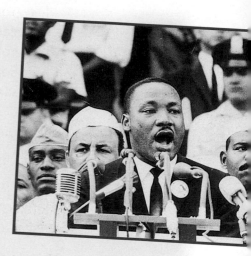

Your task is to prepare and deliver a formal speech lasting about one minute based on the idea of 'I have a dream'. Work on your own or with a partner and develop a speech that you could share between you. Your subject is:

> The kind of world I would like to see in the future.

You need to think about the things you feel are wrong with the world and what you would like to see happen to make the world, or this country, a better place.

Step 1: Spend some time thinking about the kinds of **ideas** you would like to express. What kinds of things do you feel are wrong in the world? You might think of things such as:

> ◆ poverty and inequality   ◆ pollution   ◆ racism   ◆ sexism   ◆ cruelty.

Is there one main thing you would like to talk about or are there several? Brainstorm some ideas.

When you have thought of a good idea for a subject or subjects it is important to start to think about different things you could say about it or them. You could use a spider diagram. Here is an example:

A world without traffic fumes

No litter

Pollution

Less noise pollution

Cleaner seas with no pollution to harm sea creatures

Step 2: The next stage is to consider **a structure** for your speech. The two speeches you have seen leading up to this activity are simply paragraphed – broken down into separate stages.

> ◆ You could use the 'I have a dream' phrase. Each paragraph or section of your speech would begin: 'I have a dream that ...'
> ◆ You could work with a partner on a '**We** have a dream' speech in which you each take sections.
> ◆ You could try to come up with your own memorable repeated phrase. Something like: *'The world will be a better place when ...'* You could use the same word, 'Let', as Nelson Mandela did: *'Let there be a world in which ...'*

You will need five or six separate sections.

Step 3: Think about the kind of **language** you will use. Speech makers think about how to make their 'message' stand out by using memorable examples of language and a lot of repetition – just as Nelson Mandela did in his speech on page 164.

Step 4: Your speech should last for about a minute and be scripted in some way. You could have the full script of your speech in front of you. But remember, as you deliver your speech it is important to establish eye contact with your audience. So you could learn your speech and deliver it from memory or use prompt cards. Re-read the advice in Activity 2, Step 4.

Step 5: As you listen to other people's speeches pay particular attention to those made by the members of your small group. Listen for evidence that they used some of the ideas for effective speech-making that you have worked on in this unit.

Step 6: When you have all delivered your speeches, sit back in your small group and feed back to each other about how effective the speeches have been. What were the strengths and in what ways could the speeches heve been improved? Focus on:

◆ language: what kinds were used?
◆ structure: was there some sense of sequence?
◆ relationship with audience: did the speaker have eye contact with the audience?

This unit will help you to:

◆ develop and compare different interpretations of dramatic scenes

◆ convey action, character and atmosphere when performing scenes

◆ use dramatic techniques to explore ideas

◆ consider the range of dramatic techniques that can be used.

Blood Brothers

Blood Brothers by Willy Russell is a musical play. It is about twin boys, Eddie and Mickey, who are separated at birth. Their mother Mrs Johnston (The Mother) is a poor cleaner who struggles to make ends meet. A rich woman, Mrs Lyons, persuades Mrs Johnston to hand over one of the twins and takes Eddie. The two boys grow up in the same area but in very different households. They meet without realising how they are related and, at the age of eight, become best friends and 'blood brothers'.

Below is Act 2 scene 9 from the play. Mrs Lyons has moved to a new district so that Eddie won't meet Mickey.

Work in small groups of four or five. Two of the group should read the parts of Mrs Lyons and Eddie. Read through the scene fairly quickly before looking at the activity that follows it.

Act 2 Scene 9

Birdsong. **The Mother** [Mrs Johnson] *watches them for a moment before she exits.*

	Mrs Lyons	Well Edward, do you like it here?
	Eddie	(*unenthusiastic*) It's very nice.
	Mrs Lyons	(*bending and pointing*) Look Edward … look at those cows …
5		and those trees. Oh Edward, you're going to like it so much out here, aren't you?
	Eddie	Yes. Are you feeling better now, Mummy?
	Mrs Lyons	Much better darling. Oh look, Edward … look, look at those birds … look at that lovely black and white one …
10	**Eddie**	(*immediately covering his eyes*) Don't Mummy, don't … don't look …
	Mrs Lyons	Edward!
	Eddie	It's a magpie. Never look at one magpie. It's one for sorrow.
	Mrs Lyons	Edward, that's just a silly superstition.
15	**Eddie**	It's not, it's not, Mickey told … me …
	Mrs Lyons	Edward, I think we can forget the silly things that Mickey says.

Eddie		I'm going inside, I want to read.
Mrs Lyons		Edward, children take time to adapt to new surroundings. But you soon won't even remember
20		that you once lived somewhere else. In a few weeks you'll forget him – Mickey. (*She smiles at him and nods. They stand together for a moment, surveying the land before them.*)
Eddie		What's that Mummy?
25 **Mrs Lyons**		(*craning to see*) What?
Eddie		There … look … below the hill.
Mrs Lyons		What? Oh those houses? That's the beginning of a council estate. But we've arranged with the gardener, he's going to plant a row of poplars
30		down at the end of the paddock there. Once they're in we won't even be able to see that estate. Oh, I love it out here. I feel secure here. I feel warm and safe. Once the trees are planted we won't even see that estate. (*She beams a smile at*
35		*him as they turn and head for the house.*)

*from **Blood Brothers** by Willy Russell*

Interpreting and acting the character of Mrs Lyons

Activity 1 🆆🆂

1 Explore the following in your small group.

   a Does the writer want you to see Mrs Lyons as 'posh'?

   ◆ Find words she uses which could be called 'posh'.

   ◆ Find things she says that shows her attitudes/ideas are 'posh'.

   b Does Mrs Lyons have a good relationship with her son? Focus on:

   ◆ what she and Eddie **say**

   ◆ what they **do** in this scene. (The words in *italics* in brackets are 'stage directions'. These are advice from the writer about what characters **do** on stage.)

2 Here is one way of looking at Mrs Lyons.

> *She is extremely 'posh': she talks in a posh way, she's a snob and she treats her son as though he needs to be protected from the real world. She's not a very likeable character and the relationship between her and her son isn't very good.*

   a In your group discuss how you could read the scene in this way.

   ◆ How might she speak? Which 'posh' words could you emphasise to show what she is like? What tone of voice could she use?

   ◆ How might Eddie speak to her to show that he isn't very happy?

   ◆ What might she and Eddie do to show there is tension in their relationship? For example, when she says 'I love it out here', what could Eddie do to show he feels differently?

   b When you have discussed these points, rehearse a reading of this scene.

3 Here is a different way of looking at Mrs Lyons.

> *She is a caring woman who only wants the best for her son. Although she is quite well spoken she isn't a snob; it's just the way she talks. Her son is upset at the move of house, but he loves her and she loves him.*

In your group, discuss how you could read the scene to show this different view. Follow the same stages you explored in your previous interpretation.

4 When you have been through the two ways of looking at Mrs Lyons, discuss which of the two:

   a seems to fit the evidence of the text best   b is the most entertaining.

Choose one of your versions to act to the class. When you have finished, your 'audience' should be able to tell you whether your version was the one in which Mrs Lyons was likeable or not and how they knew.

Mickey and The Mother

Remain in your small groups and read the next scene of *Blood Brothers*. There are two characters: The Mother and Mickey. A couple of years after Mrs Lyons and Eddie moved to be away from Mrs Johnston and Mickey, Mrs Johnston is being re-housed to the council estate near to where Mrs Lyons lives. As the scene is read, think about the ways in which this scene is similar to, but different from, the previous one. Use the following table to jot down ideas.

	What is similar	What is different
The mother/son relationship		
The ways the mothers behave		
The ways the characters speak		

Act 2 scene 10

As they [Mrs Lyons and Eddie] *exit we see* **Mickey** *and* **The Mother** *enter, each carrying a suitcase.* **The Mother** *is vigorously taking in the fresh air and leading the way as* **Mickey** *struggles with the case, behind her. He is now twelve.*

Mickey   (*stopping and pointing*) Is that our new house there Mam?

The Mother (*looking*) Where?

Mickey   There … look, you can just see it behind that row of trees.

The Mother (*laughing*) Mickey … give over will you. The Corporation doesn't build houses like that. That's a private house son. (*She points in the other direction.*) No … look, down the hill … that's where ours is. Look. Oh … son, isn't it nice out here? Eh?

Mickey   It's like the country isn't it, Mam?

The Mother Eh, we'll be all right here, son. Away from the muck and dirt. And the bloody trouble. You can breathe out here, Mickey. Hey, I could dance. Couldn't you?

Mickey   (*alarmed*) What?

The Mother (*grabbing him*) Come on … (*She lilts the tune and waltzes him around the road as he protests vigorously.*)

Mickey   Mother … Mother put me down will you. (*Breaking away, leaving his mother to dance alone, looking around and checking that nobody saw him then watching his mother as she dances. Slowly a huge smile breaking across his face.*)

The Mother And what are you laughing at? I used to be a good dancer you know. A very good dancer in fact.

Mickey   I'm not laughing. I'm smiling. I haven't seen you happy like this for ages.

The Mother Well I'm happy now. You never know, Mickey, play your cards right, we might have tea from the chippie.

Mickey (*picking up his case as does* **The Mother**) Ooh, can we, Mam, can we?

The Mother Come on, come on. Hey, Jesus, where's the others? Where's our Sammy and the others?

Mickey They went into that field, Mam.

The Mother Which field?

Mickey (*pointing*) That field.

The Mother (*craning, horror stricken, shouting*) Sammy, Sammy get off that cow before I bleedin kill you. Oh Jeez, what's our Donna Marie put her sodding foot in? Sammy, get hold of her … wipe it off … oh … come on, Mickey … come on …
(*Exit.*)

from **Blood Brothers** *by Willy Russell*

Activity 2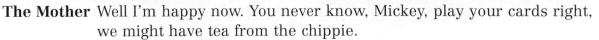

1 Compare your notes with others in your small group. Share ideas and complete a small-group table.

2 This scene is similar to the first one you read: a mother and son are moving into a new area. Is the **atmosphere** of the two scenes the same? Look at the following list of words and decide which best describe the **atmosphere** in each scene.

◆ happy	◆ sad	◆ serious	◆ tense	◆ angry
◆ loving	◆ comic	◆ gloomy	◆ cold	◆ warm

When you have chosen the words that best describe each scene, write down the evidence from the play to support your opinion.

3 What has the writer done to make the two female characters different? Copy and complete the following chart with more ideas. It has been started for you.

	Mrs Lyons	The Mother
How do they speak differently?	She is very 'correct': she calls her son 'Edward' rather than using a shortened form	She calls her son 'Mickey' rather than using 'Michael'
How do they behave differently?	She is quite serious	She fools around: she dances in public
How do the sons react differently?	Eddie seems quite tense – he's upset by the magpie	Although Mickey is embarrassed by his 'dancing' mother, he's quite happy and relaxed

Directing and acting both scenes

A director might have various ideas for how scenes 9 and 10 should be acted. You are going to explore how one director imagines the characters. This director would like the differences between the two families to be made obvious. She wants the audience to find The Mother likeable and fun and Mrs Lyons snobbish and not very likeable. These are the differences to be made obvious.

> ◆ The difference in social class – rich/poor, posh/down to earth.
> ◆ The difference between the two mothers. Mrs Johnston is the 'real' mother and the audience is to be attracted to her, whereas Mrs Lyons is a 'false' mother and the audience is to find her unsympathetic and snobbish.
> ◆ Eddie is to be seen as rather babyish because of the influence of Mrs Lyons, whereas Mickey is a more likeable, independent character.

Activity 3 ⓦ

1 Use a chart like the one below to help you think about how you could achieve what the director wants. Work in your small group.

What the director wants	What we could do
Differences in social class to be highlighted. Mrs Lyons and Eddie are well off; the Mother and Mickey are much more 'common'.	Make Mrs Lyons and Eddie talk softly and very 'correctly' – no dropping 'h' from the start of words. Their accents could be 'posh'. On the other hand, The Mother and Mickey …
Differences between the mothers to be highlighted so that we see how 'posh' Mrs Lyons is and how down to earth The Mother is. The Mother is seen to be a better mother figure than Mrs Lyons. Think about how they speak – their accent and tone of voice. Think about how they behave – what they do as they speak or listen.	The Mother is really struggling with what she is carrying – she has to work. Mrs Lyons, on the other hand, seems very relaxed as though she doesn't have to work.
Eddie to be seen as a bit of a 'mummy's boy', whereas Mickey is more fun, has a bit more about him. What could the boys do that would show how they are different?	Mickey could talk louder – he's got a bit of character. He could look untidier.

2　When you have discussed these points and made some notes, decide who will read which part and then read through both scenes trying to follow the ideas you noted down.

3　Now explore **actions**. Actions can completely change the meanings of words. For example: at the beginning of the first scene, Mrs Lyons asks Eddie if he is going to enjoy it in their new house and he answers 'Yes'. If he smiles at her genuinely when he says it, it will mean 'yes'. But if his back is turned towards her and the audience sees that he says it through clenched teeth, then it would mean 'no'.

You need to decide what each character should do:

| ◆ when they speak | ◆ when the other character is speaking. |

You could think about:

- ◆ the expression on their face
- ◆ where they look
- ◆ how they stand or move.

4　As two of you read the parts in one scene, the others in the group should act as directors, advising the two 'actors' about what they could be doing as they speak and respond. Then change the parts for the next scene and do the same.

5　Rehearse your two scenes and show them to the rest of the class.

Producing your own drama texts

Blood Brothers is a musical play that explores a range of issues about upbringing, families and the differences between rich and poor. *Stone Cold* is a novel that explores issues to do with homelessness.

Link, a teenage boy, has become homeless. What follows is his description of the circumstances that led to his becoming homeless. As you read, focus on trying to get Link's story clear in your mind.

p.204

My Fascinating Life

Yes.

Born March 20th, 1977, in Bradford, Yorkshire to Mr & Mrs X. We were a family, you know – as happy as most, till Dad ran off with a receptionist in 1991, when I was fourteen and at the local comp. This mucked up my school work for

5 quite a while, but that's not why I ended up like this. No. Vincent's to blame for that. Good old Vince. Mum's boyfriend. You should see him. I mean, Mum's no Kylie Minogue – but Vincent. He's about fifty for a start, and he's one of these old dudes that wear cool gear and try to act young and it doesn't work because they've got grey hair and fat bellies and they just make themselves pathetic. And as if that's

10 not enough, Vince likes his ale. I suppose Dad must've been a bit of a bastard in his way, but at least he wasn't a boozer. You should see the state Vincent's in when he and Mum come home from the club. He's got this very loud laugh – laughing at nothing, if you know what I mean – and he stands there with his arm round Mum, slurring his words as he tells me to call him Dad. Dad. I wouldn't call that fat

15 pillock Dad if he was the last guy on earth. And the one thing that really bugs me is the way he leers at Mum and comes out with this very suggestive stuff about going to bed and rounding off a decent night. In all the years Dad was with us, I never once knew him to mention sex in my hearing, or even hint at it. This slob leers and winks and nudges with one eye on me to see how I'm taking it, and Mum just

20 laughs and shoves him and says ooh, you are a one. It makes me puke.

He's changed her. That's one of the things I hate him for. She used to be one of those quiet people who are satisfied with the daily routine of their lives. She hardly ever went out at night – she didn't seem to want to. She was wrapped up in her family, I guess. She was always there when you needed her and I think she loved

25 us. Me and Carole, I mean.

Oh, I know how it sounds, me going on like this about Mum as though she wasn't entitled to a life of her own. Of course she's entitled, but what I'm saying is, why Vince?

Carole's my sister, by the way. She's four years older than me and she always

30 spoiled me, and when good old Vince moved in and Mum started changing it was Carole who made life bearable for me. It was bad, but I could stand it with her

there to support me. Then one night when Mum was working late, something happened between Carole and Vince. I didn't understand it then and she never told me anything, but I've a fair idea now what it must've been. Anyway, she said
35 something to Mum and they had this flaming row and it ended with Carole walking out of the house. She moved in with her boyfriend and I was on my own. I stuck it out till I finished school, but that was it. I'd got five GCSEs, which was a miracle when you remember what was going on at home, but I couldn't get a job and there's no government money for school-leavers. You're supposed to be on a
40 training scheme, but there aren't enough places and I didn't get one. I'm sure Mum would've supported me till I found something, but it wasn't long before Vince started on at me about living on his money. I wasn't living on his money – I'd have topped myself first. It was Mum's money, but he went on and on, getting nastier and nastier, and one night when I'd been with my mates he locked me out
45 of the house. It wasn't even his house but he locked the door and wouldn't let Mum open it. I went round to Carole's and she let me spend the night, and when I got home next morning Vince started slapping me around the head for going off and worrying Mum. If you happen to know anybody who's looking for a one hundred per cent out-and-out bastard, I can let him have Vince's address.
50 　　Anyway, that's how he was with me and I guess Mum's scared of him because she didn't stick up for me, so I left. You'd have left too, in my place. Anybody would. It's called making yourself homeless. And so here I am sitting in this doorway which is now my bedroom, hoping some kind punter will give me a bit of small change so I can eat.
55 　　Good, eh?

*from **Stone Cold** by Robert Swindells*

Activity 4 ⓦⓢ

In groups of four or five, discuss which character you would blame for what happened to Link. Make notes, using a table like the one below.

The character	What they did
Link	He seems to have 'got in the way of' his mum and her new boyfriend. He walked out – he didn't have to.
Vince	He drank. He made life very difficult for Link. He hit him. He locked him out.
Link's mother	She puts up with Vince. She doesn't stand up to him.

Using drama to explore an issue

You are now going to explore the issue of homelessness in a more extended piece of drama. Your small group of four or five will produce a piece of drama in two parts.

Part 1: The events that led to a young person becoming homeless

Part 2: What that person's experience of being homeless was like

The two parts of the drama should be planned one at a time, following the stages outlined in Activities 5 and 6.

Activity 5 ⓦ

Part 1: The events that led to a young person becoming homeless

Step 1: Brainstorm a few ideas. You have already looked at Link's story of how he became homeless. Think about the kinds of pressures there can be on young people:

a family/family break-up?   **c** bullying?

b school pressures?   **d** getting in with a group of troublemakers?

Step 2: Now invent a character, a young person. Give the character a name. Then, working together, make up a story about that character based on your chosen idea. Note down a rough outline of the story. Here is an example:

> A teenager's dad loses his job and it causes tension in the family: there are arguments about money.
>
> Eventually there is a blazing row between teenager and dad, which leads to the dad striking the teenager.
>
> The teenager starts to get into trouble at school, which leads to further arguments.
>
> The teenager is sent home from school for misbehaviour and decides to run away.

Step 3: Now write down some details on the following.

a The important people in your character's life. This should be a very small number – only two or three. They could be family, friends, teachers – it depends on the story.

b Two or three significant 'events': events that played a large part in what happened to your character.

Step 4: Now you need to decide how to dramatise your story. It should be brief: a maximum of **five minutes**. Here are some dramatic methods you can use.

a Act out short scenes – dramatising the important events in the character's life that led to the person leaving home.

b Have characters talking to the audience in role, telling them their side of the story.

c Use a narrator to talk to the audience and introduce different scenes and/or characters.

Step 5: Think about your performance.

a How will the audience know who is who? Will characters introduce themselves or will they use names early on? Remember, in your small group each of you may have to play several different parts.

b How will you make the differences between characters obvious for the audience? How will they speak differently and behave differently? Think back to the work you did on *Blood Brothers* and how to make characters different. You could vary language according to the character:

> ◆ use slang for the young homeless
> ◆ use a different kind of speech for, say, any parents involved
> ◆ use particular terms for any professionals or experts you create. For example a police officer talking about the problems faced by young people might use vocabulary such as 'assault', 'caution', 'trespass', 'the rights of shopkeepers'.

Step 6: When you have decided on your story and how to dramatise it you should start to rehearse the scenes to make sure they fit within the time limit.

Activity 6

Part 2: What that person's experience of being homeless was like

Step 1: First make a list of some of the problems about sleeping rough, for example:

> ◆ lack of hygiene and comfort   ◆ increased risk of violence.

Step 2: When you have made a list, read the next extract from *Stone Cold* (page 180) to give you more insight into the kinds of problems faced by young people sleeping rough on the streets. It has been annotated to help you. Add further points to your list.

Stone Cold

So you pick your spot. Wherever it is (unless you're in a squat or a derelict house or something) it's going to have a floor of stone, tile, concrete or brick. In other words it's going to be [hard and cold.] It might be a bit cramped too – shop doorways often are. And remember, if it's winter you're going to be
5 [half frozen] before you even start. Anyway you've got your place, and if you're lucky enough to have a sleeping-bag you unroll it and get in.

Settled for the night? Well maybe, maybe not. Remember my first night? The Scouser? 'Course you do. He kicked me out of my bedroom and pinched my watch. Well, that sort of thing can happen any night, and there are worse
10 things. [You could be peed on] by a drunk or a dog. Happens all the time – one man's bedroom is another man's lavatory. You might be spotted by a gang of lager louts on the look-out for someone to maim. That happens all the time too, and if they get carried away you can end up dead. There are the guys who like young boys, who think because you're a dosser you'll do
15 anything for dosh, and there's the **psycho** who'll [knife you for your pack.]

So, you lie listening. You bet you do. Footsteps. Voices. Breathing, even. Doesn't help you sleep.

Then there's your bruises. What bruises? Try lying on a stone floor for half an hour. Just half an hour. You can choose any position you fancy, and
20 you can change position as often as you like. You won't find it comfy, I can tell you. You won't sleep unless you're dead drunk or **zonked on downers**. And if you are, and do, you're going to wake up with bruises on hips, shoulders, elbows, ankles and knees – especially if you're a bit thin from not eating properly. And if you do that six hours a night for six nights you'll feel
25 like you fell out of a train. [Try sleeping on concrete then.]

And don't forget the cold. If you've ever tried dropping off to sleep with cold feet, even in bed, you'll know it's impossible. You've got to warm up those feet, or lie awake. And in January, in a doorway, in wet trainers, it can be quite a struggle. And if you manage it, chances are you'll need to get up
30 for a pee, and then it starts all over again.

And those are only some of the hassles. I haven't mentioned stomach cramps from hunger, headaches from the flu, toothache, fleas and lice. I haven't talked about homesickness, depression or despair. I haven't gone into how it feels to want a girl-friend when your circumstances make
35 it virtually impossible for you to get one – how it feels to know you're [a social outcast, in fact, a non-person] to whom every ordinary everyday activity is closed.

*from **Stone Cold** by Robert Swindells*

Word bank
psycho – mentally unstable person
zonked on downers – under the effects of drugs

It's very uncomfortable.

In winter it's freezing.

Disgusting things can happen.

It's dangerous.

It's almost impossible to sleep.

You end up with no friends.

Step 3: Next you need to decide how you will dramatise the story. Look back at the dramatic methods you explored for Part 1. If you choose to have a character or characters talk directly to the audience, the character could say something like:

> *No one cares about you; they don't want to know. I remember a day a couple of weeks ago, it was a Tuesday I think – who knows – and I was starving. I only had a couple of quid. I bought a burger but I didn't have enough for a drink. Anyway I went down the park and there were some lads kicking a football about and some girls sitting on the grass chatting. I went up to them and asked if they could spare any coppers 'cause I hadn't had anything to drink for ages. They looked at me as though I'd just crawled out from a slime pit. Then one of the lads did his Sir Galahad act and asked the girls if I was bothering them; told me to clear out or he'd sort me. Same age as me they were. Didn't want to know.*

Step 4: Now think about your performance, looking back at the points you considered for Part 1.

Step 5: Rehearse Part 2. Keep it down to **five minutes** or under.

When Parts 1 and 2 are ready, show them to the rest of the class.

This unit will help you to:

◆ listen carefully and consider the kinds of skills that aid listening
◆ consider the needs of listeners
◆ contribute to work in a small group
◆ develop interviewing skills.

Developing listening skills

Listening to a long talk can be difficult for many reasons.

> It's hard to concentrate – it might be hot; there might be a wasp buzzing around.

> The talk is hard to understand.

> You don't like what is being said.

> The speaker seems boring because he/she has a dull voice or speaks very slowly with a lot of hesitation.

Listening carefully

Activity 1

This activity will help you to think about different ways of storing information you are listening to. Work with a partner. One of you is the reader and the other is the listener.

1 Each of you should write four lists of nouns. Don't let your partner see your lists. The first list should contain four words, the second five, the third six, the fourth eight. For example:

  a tree, car, frog, table
  b pen, chair, boy, light, box
  c ruler, apple, computer, train, skateboard, rope
  d mouse, shoe, television, hat, book, jacket, road, bus

2 The **listener** isn't allowed to write any notes as he or she listens but will have to say the lists back to the reader. The listener needs some ways of remembering the items in the list. Here are some things you could do to help you.

> ◆ Fix pictures of the different items in the list in your mind.
> ◆ Build up a simple story – for example, there was a tree, a car drove into it, a frog dropped out of the tree and landed on a table.
> ◆ Remember the initial letter – a tree T, a car C, a frog F, a table T: TCFT.

3 **Reader**: read out the four words on your first list. After a brief pause, read out the five words on the second list. Read them quite slowly with only a second between each item.
   Listener: listen carefully to the lists of words as they are spoken. Try to use one of the suggested methods outlined above. When the reader has finished, speak the words back.

4 Then the reader reads the third and fourth lists with a brief pause between each. Keep a score of how many words the listener remembers each time.

5 Now swap over and let the listener become the reader.

When you have finished, swap ideas for what the listeners can do to try to fix details in their memories. Which of the suggested methods worked best?
Do you have your own method to help you remember things you have heard?

Listening for particular information

When you are reading for information you sometimes **skim** a piece of text. You skim a text when you are *reading it to get a general impression of what it is about*. It can be similar with listening. In a lesson, for example, when introducing a new topic a teacher will often begin by talking in general about that topic. You won't be listening for any particular piece of information, you will be listening to get an overall idea of the subject.

On the other hand, you might be looking for a particular piece of information. In those circumstances, if reading, you **scan** the text *looking for the particular piece of information* and pay little attention to the rest of the text. So with listening: sometimes, you might be asked to listen for something in particular, such as information about a specific task.

The following activity will give you the opportunity to practise listening for particular information.

Activity 2

There are two lists of words below, A and B.

In list A there are some fruits, colours, boys' names, girls' names and things to do with computers. In list B there are some pieces of furniture, school subjects, clothes, things to eat and some sports.

Work in pairs. One of you will listen, while the other one reads.

1 **Reader**: choose a list. Ask your partner to close his (or her) book. Tell your partner which things you want him to listen for. For example you might ask him to listen only for fruits. Then read out the entire list.

2 **Listener**: as your partner is reading the list, listen carefully for the information you have been asked to select. Then use one of the methods you practised in Activity 1 to 'fix' the things in your mind before repeating them back to your partner.

3 To make it more difficult you could ask your partner to listen for two categories.

4 When you have finished you should swap roles.

LIST A	apple	Yvette	mouse	Tony	Frank
	red	screen	keyboard	peach	brown
	John	blue	Michelle	Donna	hard disc
	Maggie	Leon	purple	software	Mike
	pear	grape	banana	green	Katy
LIST B	Maths	chair	scarf	ice-cream	rugby
	swimming	shoes	chips	RE	table
	orange	Science	wardrobe	hat	French
	netball	sausages	socks	hockey	art
	bed	rice	sofa	sweatshirt	basketball

In Activity 2 your partner told you what to listen for *before* he/she read the list. It is quite important to have a clear idea of what you are listening for. The following activity will help to show this.

Activity 3 ⓦⓢ

Work in pairs.

1 Choose, copy and complete one of the following tables while your partner copies and completes the other one.

Table A	Table B
List five animals:	List five months:
List five sports:	List five birds:
List five insects:	List five cities:
List five numbers:	List five drinks:

2 When you have completed your tables, you will each have a list of 20 words. Mix up your 20 words so that they no longer appear in categories (groups of things).

3 Then take it in turns to read your complete list to your partner. *After* you have read the list give your partner the name of the items you would like them to recall. For example, you might ask them to list the five insects.

In practising your listening skills, which suggestion for trying to 'fix' things in your memory has worked best? Discuss with your partner what has been most successful.

Listening and making notes

Sometimes it is helpful to write things down when you are listening to a talk. Because it is difficult to keep up with the speed at which people talk, it is useful to use abbreviations when you are making notes.

If you are used to sending text messages on a mobile phone you will be aware of abbreviations that you can use. For example, a single letter 'u' instead of the word 'you' can be very useful when you are writing quickly making notes and trying to listen to a speaker at the same time. Text messaging often misses out vowels and is still readable. For example, you should be able to interpret this message: Lstnng + mkng nts.

Activity 4

1 Work in a group that includes some students who are used to text messaging. Prepare a list of some of the abbreviations that are useful. Share the list with other members of the class. Remember: you need to make sure that the abbreviation is recognisable to you at a later stage. For example, if you were using first and last letters of words for abbreviations you could use 'Ty' for a day of the week and then not be sure if it is Tuesday or Thursday.

2 You already know many useful abbreviations – think of 'exams' for examinations; 'maths' for mathematics; 'hmwk' for homework. Working in your small group, decide how the following words could be abbreviated in a helpful way:

a Shakespeare	e the Houses of Parliament	i Christianity
b Romeo and Juliet	f volume	j percussion
c Sulphur dioxide	g adjective	k battle
d Photosynthesis	h longitude and latitude	l two hundred grams of self-raising flour

Another way of abbreviating is to not write in sentences. Often it is better to use bullet points, which you can list vertically. Here is an example. A class has watched a film of Shakespeare's *Macbeth* and the teacher talks to them about the opening scene. The teacher is hoping to make a few things clear about the scene:

> *The opening scene is important for a lot of reasons. The play opens with the sounds of thunder which immediately creates a threatening atmosphere and when the weird sisters or witches start to talk you get some background to what has been going on – there has been a battle. They mention Macbeth so you know that there is some connection between the witches and Macbeth.*

A student listening to this, and wanting to make notes to help remember what the teacher had said, might have written down:

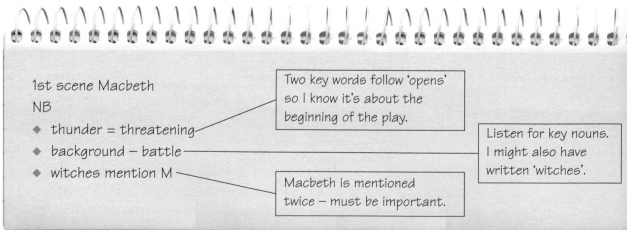

'NB' is an abbreviation of the Latin *nota bene* (note well). You can use it to mean 'this is important'.

Activity 5

Imagine that the text below was spoken to you. Make notes on the text, using bullet points and abbreviations.

> *Are there too many CCTV cameras around these days? They do a good job in helping to catch criminals. So terrorists and ordinary, innocent people have got nothing to fear from them. Most of the time you aren't even aware that they are there. But this is a free country and people should be able to go about their business without being snooped on by people who can spy on them from a long way off. Everyone is entitled to a bit of privacy.*

Compare your notes with a partner's to see if you can learn from your partner's approach.

Talking in ways that help listeners

Listening can be quite a difficult activity. It is important for speakers to organise talks in ways that make listening easier for an audience. The talk should have a clear shape. A badly prepared talk might ramble, and therefore be very boring. This is why most speakers write down their talk in some form: sometimes an outline or prompt cards, often word for word, before it is spoken. Having notes helps to give the speaker some confidence.

Understandably, many people get very nervous at the thought of giving a talk to an audience. There are things you can do to make it easier and that will contribute to a successful talk.

◆ Be well prepared. Know what you want to talk about.
◆ Try not to use 'fillers' like 'erm', 'you know'.
◆ Try to look confident. Don't fidget with anything – notes, hair, buttons, etc. Fidgeting makes you look nervous.
◆ Look at your audience.
◆ Try to control your breathing.

Activity 6 Ⓦ

This activity involves you in preparing talks that are quite straightforward so that you can concentrate on making eye contact with your audience.

1 Work with a partner.

   a Prepare a simple talk – 'My three favourite television programmes'.
   This will be a list with some reasons attached. For example, you might begin:

   > *The first programme I really like is 'The Simpsons'. I like it because it makes me laugh. The voices are so stupid. Homer is my favourite character because he's so ridiculous but loveable! Another programme I like is ...*

   You could make some prompts if it helps. For example the talk above could have had prompts like this: *1st Prog*: Simpsons: makes me laugh/voices/Homer my favourite.

   b When you have thought about what you are going to say, deliver your talk to your partner while looking into his/her eyes – across a desk, for example. If you need to look at prompts, pause before looking up and speaking again.

2 Now work alone.

   a You are going to deliver a short talk to the class in which you will try to make eye contact with as many members of the class as possible. Choose from the list below for your talk on 'My three favourite ...'

   ◆ books
   ◆ films
   ◆ places
   ◆ people
   ◆ songs.

   b Your talk should last between 30 and 60 seconds, no more. Like the talk you delivered to your partner, this one should be a list of the three things with reasons for liking them. Prepare prompts if you feel you need them, but remember to pause as you look down at them.

   c As you talk, try to look at *everyone* in the room at least once. Don't stare at them, just catch their eye. You will find that you need to talk quite slowly. When your talk is over the class will let you know if they feel you caught their eye.

Speaking clearly and avoiding 'fillers'

It is very important to speak clearly when talking to an audience. Everyone needs to be able to hear you, so be careful not to mumble in a low voice, or 'gabble' by talking too quickly.

'Fillers' are sounds like 'um', 'erm', 'uh', 'you know', 'like'. We all use them when we are thinking aloud. If you use them a lot in prepared talks it sounds as if you are not too sure of what you want to say and are having to think on the spot.

Here is an out-of-breath athlete's response when asked how he feels after a race:

> *'I'm really, you know, really happy, you know, to have won that race after all the, you know, all the training and hard work I've been through, you know, it's terrific, you know, really terrific.'*

The athlete is having to make something up on the spot – no wonder there are a lot of fillers. It shouldn't happen to the same extent in a prepared talk because you would deal with the thinking spaces at the planning stage.

Activity 7 WS

Working in groups of between four and six, you are each going to talk for one minute on a subject that you have chosen from the list below.

- ◆ My taste in music
- ◆ How I'd spend a £1 million
- ◆ A perfect Saturday
- ◆ A special interest of mine

Step 1: When you have chosen your subject, spend five minutes working out what you are going to say. Don't write out a script, but you might find it helpful to prepare some prompts.

Step 2: Each group member has to deliver his/her talk without using any 'fillers' and trying to make eye contact with everyone in the group.

Step 3: The rest of the group should make a note of how many 'fillers' are used and whether they feel the speaker made eye contact.

Step 4: When everyone has given their talk, discuss in your groups how well each person managed to avoid fillers.

Sounding confident

It helps if you can avoid 'fillers', look at your audience and speak clearly with some confidence. Your audience will be more prepared to listen to you if you seem to know what you are talking about and can speak with enthusiasm.

Activity 8

Work in groups of four or five on this activity.

Your group's task is to make a presentation. Imagine your Year group has been asked to come up with new ideas for how to raise money for charity. The Chair of the Governors has invited groups of students to submit ideas for a day of fund-raising. The Governors would like to hear the proposals before deciding which one is best. Your small group is going to:

- ◆ explore some ideas
- ◆ discuss how to present them in a confident and interesting way
- ◆ make the presentation.

Exploring ideas

Step 1: Brainstorm some ideas about different things that could be done in the day to raise money. There are some obvious things like sponsored silences or sponsored cake sales, but try to be more imaginative. When you have some ideas decide which ones you think are most interesting.

Step 2: Then discuss how your ideas could be organised: what would need to be done? If you want your ideas to be accepted then you need to show you have thought them through. For example, if you decided to have a disco how would you supervise it? Would you provide food and drink? When would it start and finish?

How to present the ideas

Each group member should have a chance to contribute to the presentation.

Step 1: Decide who will speak about which idea and what each person will have to say. Help each other make prompt cards to support you in delivering your talk.

Step 2: Remind yourselves of some important features of giving a talk: avoiding fillers; making eye contact; appearing confident.

Step 3: Have a practice run-through of the talk, stopping each other and advising if it doesn't seem to be going well.

Make your presentation to the rest of the class

When all the presentations have been made give feedback to the rest of the class about how well prepared and confident each presentation seemed.

Speaking at interviews

You have explored some of the skills required in giving talks or speeches, alone or in a group presentation. An interview is another situation where your ability to speak well and sound confident is particularly important. Interviews are occasions when people are judged.

Activity 9

1 In groups of four or five briefly share ideas on what you think happens in a job interview. If any of you have experienced one it would be useful to share your impressions of what happened.

2 Staying in your group, choose **one** of the following jobs you are all going to apply for:

> ◆ shop assistant at a local newsagent
> ◆ shop assistant at a local electrical goods/computer shop
> ◆ assistant at a local vet's
> ◆ coach of a local U14 team (you decide the sport).

3 Each person in the group will be interviewed in turn by the remaining members of the group. The questions are set out on page 192, followed by some tips on answering the questions.

4 After each group member has spoken the group will discuss the different interviewees and vote on who they think spoke most confidently.

5 Every person in the group should consider their own 'performance' and think about which areas of their speaking should be targeted for improvement.

Questions

Each group member will be asked the following basic questions.
These questions are designed to find out the kind of information the
interviewing panel would need to know.

> 1 *Good morning Miss/Mr X. Could you please tell us a little bit about yourself?*
>
> 2 *Tell us, Miss/Mr X, why you have applied for this job?*
>
> 3 *Do you have any previous experience that we should know about?*
>
> 4 *Why do you think you are the right person for this job?*

The group should add two further questions and then decide the order in which
they are going to ask them.

Answering the questions

Question 1 Think about what would interest the interview panel – where you
live, your education, your interests, how you spend your spare time.

Question 2 This obviously depends on the job. If you were applying for the
vet's assistant you would want to speak about your interest in animals. You
might talk about pets you have had or television programmes you have
watched.

Question 3 For the purposes of this activity you will make this up. If you say
you haven't worked in a shop before you can still mention experience in
handling money, or in talking to members of the public.

Question 4 Think about what qualities the job needs. For example, if you wish
to coach a team it would help if you get along with people, are reliable, know
about the sport, etc.

Appear confident

> ◆ Spend some time before the interview thinking about which qualities the
>   job requires so that you are prepared. Don't use prompts.
> ◆ Establish eye contact with the interview panel and be enthusiastic.
> ◆ Avoid too many 'fillers'.
> ◆ Speak clearly without mumbling.

Work in groups of three or four. 'Invent' a charity and prepare a presentation about it. Your presentation should be something that could be delivered to your Year group in an assembly and should last for approximately five minutes.

The charity

Charities are groups of people who raise money for and try to help deserving cases. For example, you will probably have heard of the RSPCA and know what they do. Do you know any others? Your small group will discuss and choose your invented charity.

The purpose

The purpose of your presentation is to:

◆ describe to the audience why there is a need for your charity

◆ explain to them the kinds of things your charity does.

Planning and rehearsing

It is very important that *everyone* in your small group makes a contribution that may be assessed. As a group you should follow these steps.

Step 1: Discuss the different possibilities for a charity and take a decision about which one is best. You need to think about:

◆ what your charity's aim is, e.g. to help animals or a particular group of people

◆ reasons why the charity is needed, e.g. insufficient government or state provision

◆ a list of the things your charity does

◆ whether it's a big national charity like the RSPCA, or a smaller local charity to help a particular group in your area

◆ a name for your charity.

Step 2: Discuss how you can make your assembly interesting and entertaining. Think back to some of the dramatic techniques you used in Unit 19 and the work you did on presentations in Unit 18. For example, to show why there is a need for your charity, you might:

◆ invent a little piece of drama
◆ stage an interview in front of the audience about things that have happened to you
◆ take it in turns to tell a story about something that has happened to you, or something that the charity has done for you.

When you have thought of some ideas you should try them out and discuss which ones seem to work best.

Step 3: Decide on a structure for your assembly. For example, you might decide to begin with one student making an opening presentation, introducing the charity. This could be followed by a brief piece of drama exploring the need for the charity. To conclude, another student might draw out the 'message' of the story and give the audience some ideas to think about.

Step 4: As you discuss ideas and rehearse you should remember the work you did in Unit 20 about working together with other people. This stage of your work is as important as the final presentation.

The presentation
When you have discussed and tried out your ideas, give your presentation to the rest of the class. The presentation should build on the skills you developed in Unit 18. Remember:

◆ to use language in ways that will attract your audience
◆ to use standard English, as your presentation is quite formal
◆ the importance of eye contact.

Section F ◆ Words: spelling strategies and vocabulary
Introduction

The following units will help you to:

◆ revise and develop strategies to improve your spelling

◆ revise and remember the spellings you use frequently

◆ investigate more difficult spellings

◆ remember spelling rules and conventions to improve your written work.

First, find out how well you can spot spelling mistakes.

How well do you spell?

During the drafting and redrafting stage, you should check through your written work regularly. One of the important things to watch out for is spelling errors.

Some students were asked to draft a letter to be sent home to Year 9 parents. Read their first draft and note the words that you think are spelt wrong. Next to each one, write the correct spelling. If you are unsure, you can use a dictionary.

Tommorow, Year 9 will be going on the school trip. Four teachers will be accompaning them. They are going to North Wales to do some geography feild work. Students will have opportunities to buy souvenirs and gifts for their parents.

Mid-afternoon, they will walk up a mountain, where they will complete a worksheet based on rocks. They will be able to go to the cafeteria which has a dineing area to purchase their lunchs from. They will then decend the mountain and make their way to where the coaches will be situated.

Hopefully everyone will enjoy themselfes and the trip will not be spoiled by irresponsible students.

How many incorrect words did you find? Check them against the list on the next page.

ICT This unit will help you to revise and improve your spelling.

Activity 1 Spelling tips and rules

1 Here are some mis-spelt words from the draft letter on page 195, together with a list of spelling tips and rules. Write the words in your book and match each one with the tip or rule the writer should have applied. For example, **feild = c**.

Mis-spelt words
feild
accompaning
themselfes
dineing
lunchs
decend
tommorow

Spelling rules and tips
a words ending in *–sh*, *–ch*, *–x*, *–z* or *–s*: add *–es* to make plural
b words that end in *–f* or *–fe*: change the *f* into a *v* and add either *–s* or *–es* to make plural
c '*i* before *e* unless after *c*'
d sound out every part of the word
e verbs that end in *–e*: remove the *e* before adding suffix *–ing*
f watch out for silent letters
g make sure you double the right letter in a word

2 There are always words that break these rules (known as exceptions). With a partner write down four words that break rules **b** and **c**.

3 Choose one of the rules or tips that you think will improve your spelling.
   ◆ Try to learn it.
   ◆ Write a list of words that the rule or tip will help you spell.
   ◆ Look at a recent piece of your writing. Write down the words that follow this tip or rule.

Activity 2 Mnemonics

Mnemonics help you to remember spellings by using rhymes or memorable phrases. For example:

> t o m o r r o w
> tomatoes   on   Monday   or   red   raspberries   on   Wednesday
> OR
> t h e m s e l v e s
> elves in themselves

1   Write out some mnemonics for the following words that you may come across in Science.

> ◆ **alkaline**   ◆ **cycle**   ◆ **oxygen**   ◆ **apparatus**

2   Think of three words from Science that you often spell wrong. Check their spelling, then write them down. Make up a mnemonic for each to help you spell them in future.

Activity 3 Tricky spellings

Some words make most people wonder if they are correct.

Look at these words. Choose four which make you think twice. Sound them out or make up a mnemonic. Then get a partner to test you on them.

> ◆ **necessary**   ◆ **definite**   ◆ **embarrass**   ◆ **business**
> ◆ **surprise**   ◆ **knowledge**   ◆ **height**   ◆ **alcohol**

> **Remember** Keep a note of words that you find difficult to spell. Practise three of them every day to help you to learn them.

Activity 4 Spellings in other subject areas

1   Look at these words from Maths and History. Use one or more of the above strategies to help you to learn to spell them. Shut the book and get a partner to test you on them. Then talk about which strategies you used.

> ◆ **parallel**   ◆ **recurring**   ◆ **tonne**   ◆ **disease**   ◆ **political**

2   Look at your own work in Maths and History. Pick three words that you find difficult to spell correctly. Apply one or more of the spelling strategies to them, then ask a partner to test you.

⬧ This unit will help you to learn difficult spellings by working out where a word comes from.

Activity 1 Word origins

 In Unit 1 you learned how earlier forms of English, Old English (Anglo-Saxon) and Middle English differ from Modern English which we use today.

 In pairs, write these words in three columns according to which era you think they come from. Look at pages 8–10 and 17 to find the answers.

pp.8, 10 & 17

◆ hosen	◆ moyste	◆ leofan	◆ e-mail
◆ housbondes	◆ online	◆ ealdor	◆ forheapen

Activity 2 Word families

 Word families have the same root word. Finding the root word may help you to work out the meaning of the whole word.

1 Look at the following word family. Write down the common root word.

◆ happier	◆ happily	◆ happiest

2 Now write two other word families, underlining the common root word each time. Use the dictionary to help you.

Activity 3 Root words plus prefixes and suffixes

 Often the root word has a prefix or a suffix, or even both added to it. For example:

◆ en**camp**	◆ en**camp**ment

1 'Photo' appears in many other words. In pairs, produce a chain of words like the one above based on 'photo'. Then each spend five minutes writing down as many words as you can that have 'photo' as the root word.

2 Now look in the dictionary to find more 'photo' words.

Activity 4 Root words from Latin and Greek

 Look at these Latin and Greek words. Each one is the root of lots of other words.

◆ tele = distance (G)	◆ manus = hand (L)
◆ impero = I command (L)	◆ autos = self (G)

Think of three English words which are derived from each root word. Check them in the dictionary to see if you were right. Look for others with the same root.

24 Using a dictionary and thesaurus

 This unit will help you to check spellings and expand your vocabulary.

Activity 1 Using the dictionary

Use a dictionary to check **what** words mean and **how** to spell them. Don't be afraid to use new words because you don't know how to spell them.

p.64

1 In 'Exotic dawn' on page 64 the writer conjures up an exotic place. Find these words in the passage and think about the context. Write a short definition for each.

> ◆ **dense** ◆ **trailing** ◆ **sultry** ◆ **majestic** ◆ **immense**

2 Now look them up in the dictionary. How close were you to the correct definition?

> **Beware** when using a spell-checker on a computer. What word does the computer think you are trying to spell? Use a dictionary to check the word on the computer screen means what you want it to.

Activity 2 Using a thesaurus

Rather than always using the same words, try to use a range of words with similar meanings. It will add variety and interest to your written and spoken language.

pp.48–51

1 Look up the following words in a thesaurus.

> ◆ **kid** ◆ **smart** ◆ **terrific** ◆ **jealous**

2 Now read the text of *Smart ice-cream* on page 48 in which the original words appear. Try substituting some of the words you found in the thesaurus. Which of them work? Do any of them improve the writing?

> **Remember** When using the thesaurus, check that the words you use are appropriate for the context. Ask a friend, your teacher or a parent.

Activity 3 Choosing the right words

p.64

1 Select a recent piece of your own work and choose five words that you think you could improve. Using a thesaurus, rewrite the sentences, changing some words to make them more interesting and exciting.

2 Discuss both pieces with your partner. Is the new version an improvement?

3 Write the first paragraph of a feature in a holiday magazine. Use 'Exotic dawn' as a model and describe a place you have visited. Use the thesaurus to help you find vocabulary that will tempt the reader to visit.

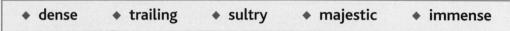

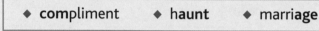 **This unit will help you to remember patterns of letters that appear in groups of words.**

Activity 1 Letter patterns

Some words can be grouped together because each contains the same spelling pattern, e.g. **c**ouch, **p**ouch, **v**ouch, **t**ouch.

1 Look at the examples below. In pairs, think of at least three words that contain the same spelling patterns. Use the dictionary to check the spellings.

> ◆ **com**pliment ◆ h**aunt** ◆ marri**age**

> **Remember** The letter pattern can appear at the beginning, in the middle or at the end of the word.

p.164

2 Look at the 'Freedom from oppression' speech on page 164. Find two groups of words that contain the regular spelling patterns '**one**' and '**ead**'.

Activity 2 Silent letters

Some words can be difficult to spell because they contain silent letters. In Unit 1, Activity 5, there is a list of 'Insults about knaves'. Knave has the silent letter pattern '**kn**'.

All the words below have a silent letter pattern. With your partner, find two more words with each letter pattern to make 'silent letter pattern groups'.

> ◆ **kn**ave ◆ li**gh**t ◆ clim**b** ◆ **h**our ◆ **gn**ome

Activity 3 Complex letter patterns

Some words contain the same sounds, but are spelt differently.

> ◆ qu**eue**, bl**ue**, y**ou** = all have the sound '**oo**'
> ◆ f**e**t**e**, l**a**t**e**, str**aight** = all have a long '**a**' sound

Can you think of any other words that have the same sound, but a different spelling pattern? Complete the following word chains.

a bead _____ _____   **b** choose _____ _____   **c** bite _____ _____

> **Remember** Watch out for these spelling patterns in your own work.

This unit will help you to work out how words are built up and so help you to spell them correctly.

A **syllable** is a unit of sound. Some words are **monosyllabic** (with one syllable, e.g. the, in, tree, dog). Others are **polysyllabic** (with more than one syllable). There are several strategies you can use to help you to spell polysyllabic words.

Activity 1 Sounding out words into syllables

The words below are often used in Geography, but are commonly mis-spelt. Sound them out. Then write each one down, showing the separate syllables. Next to it, write how many syllables each one has, e.g. **at – las** = two syllables.

- ◆ **habitat**   ◆ **settlement**   ◆ **contour**   ◆ **location**   ◆ **weather**

Activity 2 Word shape and letter patterns

Another way of learning to spell a long word, e.g. 'committed', is to visualise it.

- ◆ Look at the shape of the word – three of four letters at the end are taller.
- ◆ Find a pattern of letters – two 'm's and two 't's.

1 Spend two minutes visualising the following words used in History. Note the shape of each word. Then find a pattern of letters in each.

- ◆ **politics**   ◆ **current**   ◆ **immigrant**   ◆ **revolution**

2 Now ask a partner to check how many of these words you can spell correctly.

Activity 3 Words in words

We often learn to spell by dividing polysyllabic words up into smaller words or groups of letters, e.g. Wednesday = **Wed + nes + day**.

Split up the following polysyllabic words to help you remember how to spell them in future.

- ◆ **permanent**   ◆ **questionnaire**   ◆ **outrageous**   ◆ **possession**

Activity 4 Looking at your own work

Now look at your own writing. Find three polysyllabic words you find difficult to spell. Check them in the dictionary to make sure you know the correct spelling. Use the above strategies to remember how to spell them.

ICT This unit will help you to increase your confidence when spelling plurals and deciding when to use apostrophes.

Activity 1 Plurals

- Most words become plural by adding –s. For example, dog ⟶ dog**s**.
- Words that end with –s, –ch, –sh, –z or –x, add –es. For example, match ⟶ match**es** and box ⟶ box**es**.
- Words that end with –o after another vowel, add –s. For example, video ⟶ video**s**.
- Words that end with –o after a consonant, usually add –es. For example, tomato ⟶ tomato**es**.
- Words that end in –y after a vowel, just add –s, for example, monkeys. Whereas words that end with –y after a consonant, take off the –y and add –ies, for example, famil**ies**.

> **Remember** There are always exceptions. Some words stay the same when they become plural, e.g. **one sheep, many sheep**. Some words change unpredictably, e.g. **one mouse, many mice**.
>
> Nouns from other languages often follow different rules, e.g. **formula** ⟶ **formulas/formulae**. Science books are useful when researching these plurals.

Make the following nouns plural. Use the dictionary to help you.

> ◆ **orange** ◆ **guess** ◆ **donkey** ◆ **fisherman** ◆ **criterion** ◆ **ox**

Activity 2 Singular/plural ownership

Apostrophes are used in the following ways.
- When something belongs to a person or an object, add –'s, e.g. Sam**'s** toys.
- When something belongs to more than one person (or object), add –' (apostrophe only), e.g. ten students**'** work.
- Words that have their own plural term, e.g. men, children, revert back to the singular ownership rule (add –'s), e.g. men**'s** shoes.

Copy out the following headlines, putting the apostrophes in the right place. Use the rules listed above to help you.

BOYS LEG BROKEN IN 3 PLACES

ALL PARENTS VIEWS HEARD

ENGLANDS FIGHT FOR FOOTBALL TITLE

OLD PEOPLES HOMES IN DANGER

WOMENS RIGHTS

ICT This unit will help you to recall the difference between pairs of words that sound the same.

Activity 1 Homophones

Homophones are words that sound the same, but their meanings and spellings are different. For example:

◆ **there/their/they're** ◆ **to/too/two**

When trying to remember the difference between homophones, look carefully at the spelling and try to find ways of reminding yourself.

a allowed (meaning 'permitted')	**aloud** (as in to say 'out loud')
b threw (the past tense of 'throw')	**through** (as in 'go through the door')

1 Think of another pair of homophones. Use each one in a sentence.

2 Copy out the following sentences using the correct homophones.

a Knew homes for animals.
b I through the ball quite far.
c Have you had your hare cut?
d You're homework is written on the bored.

3 Look closely at the pairs of homophones below. Write a five-line poem called 'Going to the Beach', using *one* word from each pair of homophones. Make sure you choose the right one for your poem. Your poem need not rhyme.

◆ **see/sea** ◆ **blue/blew** ◆ **great/grate** ◆ **break/brake** ◆ **sites/sights**

WORD CONFUSION

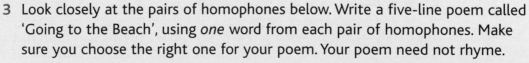

In your own writing do not use:	could of,	should of,	would of,	might of
When you should use:	could have,	should have,	would have,	might have.

This unit will help you to revise prefixes as an aid to spelling unfamiliar words.

A prefix is a group of letters that is added to the beginning of the root word.
- Most prefixes have meaning, e.g. **post** = after.
- The prefix plus the root word form a new word, which has a different meaning from the root word, e.g. war, **post**war.
- In most cases, the spelling of the root word does not change.

> For example, **predetermine:**
>
> - the prefix is **pre–**, meaning before
> - **determine** means to work out/make a decision.
>   **Predetermine** means to determine or to work out something beforehand.

Activity 1 Root words and prefixes

pp.111–113

1 In each of the sentences below, find a word which has a root word and a prefix. Underline the root word. Circle the prefix.

> a One man was going to pick two hundred pounds of cotton, and another three hundred.
> b Sounds and smells were touched with the supernatural.
> c The sounds of the new morning had been replaced with grumbles.

pp.176–177

2 From the extract from 'Stone Cold', find three words with a prefix.

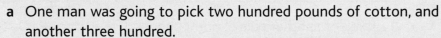

Activity 2 Antonym prefixes

Antonyms are words that have the opposite meanings to another word, e.g. big and small. An antonym prefix added to a root word creates a new word with the opposite meaning to the root word, e.g. legal, **il**legal. Some other prefixes include:

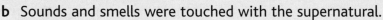

- **anti–**   - **un–**   - **im–**   - **ir–**   - **in–**   - **il–**

Make antonyms by adding one of the above prefixes to each of these words:

- **tidy**   - **climax**   - **stable**   - **mortal**   - **worthy**   - **regular**

Activity 3 More prefixes

In Maths or Science you may have come across words that have a Greek prefix, e.g. **auto**matic, **micro**scope, **kilo**gram.

1 Use your books in these subjects to find five other words that have unusual prefixes.

2 Use the dictionary to help you to work out the meaning of the prefixes in these words.

ICT This unit will help you revise suffixes as an aid to spelling unfamiliar words.

A suffix is a group of letters added to the end of the root word. When this happens:

◆ the spelling of the root word may change e.g. use**less**, pity/pit**iless**

◆ the new word will have a different meaning, e.g. fear ⟶ fear**ful**

◆ if the root is a verb, some suffixes will change it into a different part of speech, e.g. explode ⟶ explo**sion**, explo**sive**, explo**sively**.

Activity 1 Finding suffixes

The following are suffixes:

◆ –ly	◆ –sion	◆ –ity	◆ –ment	◆ –tion	◆ –ed
◆ –er	◆ –ery	◆ –able	◆ –ing	◆ –ful	◆ –es

pp.82–83

1 Investigate suffixes in the text 'All Points North' on pages 82–83. Find and write down ten words that use four of the different suffixes listed above.

2 Look at the words you have chosen. Did the root word change its spelling when a suffix was added? If so, in what way?

3 How has the suffix changed the meaning of any of your chosen words?

4 Look at a recent piece of your own work and write down the words where you have used a suffix. Have you used any suffixes that are not listed above?

Activity 2 Doubling consonants

Consonants are sometimes doubled when you add *–ing*, *–ed*, or *–er* to the word.

Rule When a word:
◆ has one syllable ◆ has a short vowel sound (e.g. tip) ◆ ends with a single consonant which is not an x or a y, double the consonant before adding *–ing*, *–ed* or *–er*, e.g.   ◆ chat = chatting   ◆ can = canned   ◆ big = bigger.

pp.78–79

1 Read lines 1–15 of 'Chinese Cinderella' on pages 78–79. Find three words in which the consonant has been doubled before adding *–ing* or *–ed*.

2 Look over a recent piece of your own writing. Check all the words ending in *–ing*, *–ed* and *–er*. Apply the above rule. Have you spelt these words correctly? Correct them if they are wrong.

Activity 3 Word endings

Complete the table below, adding a suffix to change the role of each word. Take care! Different words need different suffixes.

root word	verb	adjective	adverb
decide	decide	decisive	decisively
know			
hope			

Activity 4 Words that have both a suffix and a prefix

Some words consist of suffix + *root word* + prefix,

e.g. **un**_necessari_**ly**.

In this example, the spelling of the root word changed when the suffix was added.

1   Below is a list of root words and a list of pairs of prefixes and suffixes. Each pair will fit round one of the root words to make a longer word. Match each root with a pair and write out the complete new word. Check the dictionary, in case the root word changes its spelling.
    For example: happy (un + ly) = **un**_happi_**ly** (y becomes i)

1 found	**a** in + ly
2 stretch	**b** un + fully
3 elegant	**c** dis + ed
4 mercy	**d** pro + ly
5 order	**e** out + ed

2   Work in pairs. Decide whether the new words are verbs, adverbs or adjectives.

> **Remember** If the prefix ends with the same letter as the root word, it isn't necessary to lose one of the letters, e.g. **un**natural or **ir**regular.

31 Reviewing your progress

 ICT **This unit will help you to revise what you have learned about spelling.**

Activity 1 Review of learning

Think carefully about what you have learned from these spelling units.

- ◆ What rules and tips have you learned that will help your future writing?
- ◆ When might you use a dictionary or thesaurus to improve your writing?

Activity 2 Reviewing errors

1 Use your written work from a variety of subjects to create a personal vocabulary book. Include the correct spellings of words you struggle to spell or regularly spell incorrectly. Ask someone to test you on these words often.

2 Look at your recent spelling errors in at least two subjects. Are there any patterns? Learn the rules and make up memory aids to avoid these errors in the future.

Activity 3 Word perfect targets

1 Identify an area, covered by one of the units in this spelling section, in which you want to improve. Set yourself a spelling target. Apply the strategies in the unit every day and review your progress at the end of the week.

2 Check a piece of your own writing. Note the words where suffixes have been added. Check the spellings of these words and change any that have been mis-spelt.

3 Put an apostrophe in each of the following sentences to ensure that they are correctly punctuated.

- ◆ Ryans favourite sport is football. ◆ I cant go shopping until Saturday.
- ◆ Ten students work showed lots of improvement.

4 Think of three homophones that often confuse you. Devise three strategies to help you identify the difference between them and use them in the correct context.

Activity 4 Keep checking

1 Look carefully at the last two written pieces in your History and Geography books. Are the apostrophes, homophones and spellings correct?

2 Set yourself two targets to improve your spelling in these subject areas and try to meet these targets for the next week. For example,

- ◆ to use mnemonics
- ◆ to check, in the dictionary, any words you are unsure of.